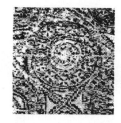

A Matter
of Self-Esteem
and Other Stories

11/5/01

For Glafyra,
with my best wishes.

Roser

A Matter
of
Self-Esteem
and Other Stories

CARME RIERA

Translated by ROSER CAMINALS-HEATH
with HOLLY CASHMAN

HM

HOLMES & MEIER
New York /London

Published in the United States of America 2001 by
Holmes & Meier Publishers, Inc.
160 Broadway • New York, NY 10038
www.holmesandmeier.com

This book was published with the assistance of the
Board of Associates of Hood College.

This book has been printed on acid-free paper.

Designed by Brigid McCarthy

Library of Congress Cataloging-in-Publication Data
Riera, Carme.
    [Qüestió d'amor propi. English]
    A matter of self-esteem and other stories / Carme Riera; translated
    by Roser Caminals-Heath; with Holly Cashman.
        p. cm.
    Contents: A matter of self-esteem—Mon semblable, mon frère—
    Against love in company—The seduction of genius—Report—
    Surprise at Sri Lanka—Recipe book.
    ISBN 0-8419-1411-7 (cloth)
    I. Caminals-Heath, Roser. II. Cashman, Holly. III. Title.

PC3942.28.I37 Q4713 2001
849'.9354—dc21
                                                      00-047263

Manufactured in the United States of America

To Francesc, always

"To love human beings is ignoble
bondage, but most ignoble of all
is to love one's self!"

JAIME GIL DE BIEDMA

Contents

Preface

WE STARTED THIS PROJECT in 1994. At the time, of all the works by Carme Riera still unavailable in English, "Qüestió d'amor propi" was the most important. In addition to its intrinsic quality, its interest lies in the fact that it marks a turning point in Riera's development between her early short fiction and her 1995 full-fledged novel, *Dins el darrer blau* (In the Last Blue of the Sky).

Riera's narrative is interspersed with literary references that sometimes present difficulties for the translator. Book titles and names of magazines occur so frequently that, for the sake of readability, we have provided English translations; only the names of a few national newspapers appear in Spanish.

As we mention in the Introduction, Carme Riera herself wrote "Qüestió d'amor propi" both in Catalan and Castilian within a short period of time. Given this fact and the virtuosity of her Castilian prose, we have treated her as a bilingual writer and based our translation on the Spanish version; thus, the characters' names in "A Matter of Self-Esteem" appear in Castilian instead of Catalan. Working with these texts, therefore, we have gained exposure to the author's entire linguistic range: Castilian, Catalan, and her native variety of the latter, Majorcan.

The rest of the stories come from her latest collection, *Contra l'amor en companyia i altres relats* (Against Love in Company and Other Stories) published in 1991. Our criteria in making the selection were, aside from literary merit, the consistency of the subject matter and, to some extent, the presence of humor, one of Riera's trademarks. This volume, given its presentation, length, and topical relevance, is equally suited to the classroom and to the general reader.

In any translation process there are identical amounts of certainty and uncertainty: the certainty that, no matter how accurate and inspired the translator may be, she will fall short of the original; the uncertainty of how close she may come and whether it is close enough. Every author is a challenge and Riera is no exception. One particular difficulty in her case is the use of Majorcan in the story "Recipe Book." Given the impossibility of capturing colloquial Majorcan speech in English, we aimed for an American cultural equivalent; if Riera's Maria sounds like an ordinary wife from a small town in Majorca, our Maria sounds, say, like a rural wife in Tennessee. Another problem for the translator is to adapt Riera's long-winded sentences, often filled with commas, to English syntax, which relies on shorter sentences divided by periods or semicolons. We have made a conscious decision to maintain the original structures whenever possible; for this reason, the reader may find more subordinate clauses set off by commas than is typical in English.

As always in this type of undertaking we should thank a good number of people. We hope, however, that all of them will feel included if we simply name our author, Carme Riera, who generously gave her time and insights one sunny afternoon by the Mediterranean. To Carme Riera and to everyone who has made our task pleasant, our deepest thanks.

ROSER CAMINALS-HEATH

Introduction

CARME RIERA, acclaimed for her rich, intricate prose and for the originality of her subjects, is unquestionably one of the major contemporary authors in Spain. Her wide range of topics, refined style, and substantial body of work merit recognition outside her own country. Born in 1949 on the Mediterranean island of Majorca, Riera earned her undergraduate and graduate degrees in Spanish at the University of Barcelona. In 1988 her essay on the group of poets known as the Barcelona School, which had been the topic of her doctoral dissertation, won the Anagrama Essay Award. As a professor at Barcelona's Autonomous University, she specializes in Spanish Literature of the Golden Age, which accounts for the numerous allusions to the classics in her work.

In the earlier stage of her career, Riera was known mainly for her collections of short stories: *Te deix, amor, la mar com a penyora* (I Leave You, My Love, the

Sea as a Token), 1975; *Jo pos per testimoni les gavines* (I Offer the Seagulls as a Witness), 1977; and *Epitelis tendríssims* (Very Tender Epitheliums), 1981. However, she soon revealed herself as an important novelist. In 1980, *Una primavera per a Domenico Guarini* (A "Primavera" for Domenico Guarini) was awarded the Prudenci Bertrana Prize; nine years later *Joc de miralls* (Mirror Images) received the Ramon Llull Prize. All these titles have been published in English, either separately or in anthologies. A more recent novel, *Dins el darrer blau* (In the Last Blue of the Sky), 1994, which deals with the last *Auto da Fe* of the Inquisition against the Jews in Majorca in the late seventeenth century, swept away the National Award in Narrative and the Josep Pla, Creixells, and Lletra d'Or Prizes.

Although these works originally appeared in Catalan, the author's native language, many of them have been translated into Castilian, the national language of Spain. In the case of "Qüestió d'amor propi" (A Matter of Self-Esteem), both versions are by the author herself and came out almost simultaneously, in 1987 and 1988.

Undoubtedly Carme Riera's choice to write in Catalan, despite the fact that her style in Castilian is equally polished, has narrowed her audience; but her decision was based on personal conviction, fueled by the ban on regional languages imposed by the dictatorship of Francisco Franco that followed the Civil

War (1936–1939). Under Franco's rule, which lasted almost forty years, it was forbidden to teach Galician, Basque, and Catalan in schools or to use them for public discourse. The regime scorned them as lesser, lower-class languages, regardless of their distinctive grammatical rules and rich literary traditions harking back to the Middle Ages. After the death of Franco in 1975, these languages experienced a resurgence and gained full status among the printed and visual media. It is not surprising that many authors have taken advantage of the new democratic freedom by writing in their native tongues. Catalan, spoken not only in the northeastern region of Catalonia, but also in Valencia, Majorca, and parts of southern France, has undergone a true revival, thanks in part to the large number of publishing houses located in Barcelona, the capital of Catalonia. In "A Matter of Self-Esteem" (Qüestió d'amor propi) Riera takes pride in her linguistic and cultural background, frequently referring to such poets as Ausias March (1397–1459) or Jordi de Sant Jordi (1385–1424), thus helping to pass on a long-standing heritage.

The Catalan boom, contemporary with the women's movement in Spain, has bred in its midst a whole generation of native women writers. Like Riera, these authors grew up under Franco's rule or in exile, as persecuted Spaniards (the topic of the Catalan exile is treated quite humorously in "Against Love in Company" [Contra l'amor en companyia], which appears in this collection).

Novelists and short story writers such as Montserrat Roig, Esther Tusquets, Maria Antonia Oliver, Anna Maria Moix, and Maria Mercè Roca have flourished over the past twenty years; in addition, some of these Catalan writers have branched out into literary criticism, like Riera and Roig, and into the publishing business, like Tusquets. The works of this group of authors convey a competence and confidence that allow them to explore new stylistic possibilities and subject matter, such as self-actualization; the search for sexual satisfaction; frustration and depression; dependence on husbands, fathers, and lovers; agoraphobia; pregnancy; and lesbianism.

According to Kathleen McNerney, editor of *On Our Own Behalf: Women's Tales from Catalonia*, Riera addresses "the difficulties of women's lives and feminist issues in original and refreshing ways without sacrificing such literary qualities as lyricism, imagery, suspense, style and elegance."[1]

Perhaps we may best describe her as an independent-minded feminist with a personal voice and an individual sensibility. Much of her fiction does focus on the lives and experiences of women, young and old, developing a wide range of female characters, from the intellectually sophisticated but emotionally naive Angela of "A Matter of Self-Esteem," to the plain and domestic Maria or Marieta of "Recipe Book" (Quadern de receptes), and the seamstress-poetess Coral of "Against Love in Company". In "A Matter of Self-Esteem," Angela bemoans the fact that Spanish literature has rarely chosen women over thirty as its heroines and that as a rule older women are caricatured and portrayed negatively. Riera, on the other hand, breaks this convention and allows her mature characters to experience passion. Autumnal love, however, almost always leads her heroines to disillusionment: In "A Matter of Self-Esteem," Angela is misused, sexually and intellectually, by an egotistic and unscrupulous male writer; in "Surprise at Sri Lanka" (Sorpresa a Sri Lanka), the seasoned journalist finally realizes that the young lover she has met on her vacation is yet another comfort provided by her fancy hotel. On the other hand, unconventional forms of female sexuality, such as autoeroticism ("Against Love in Company") are presented, with candor and understanding, as alternatives to romantic love.

Riera's women come alive not only through convincing psychological characterizations, but also through the singularity and perfect pitch of their voices. It is remarkable that the same novelist who gives us Angela's lengthy, tortured letter—filled with descriptions of nature, scholarly references, and nuanced emotions—can capture the slangy, barely literate monologue on the subject of cooking given by the simple-minded Marieta. As McNerney says

Introduction

"Riera is particularly concerned with women's language, and in fact has written an article about it. She feels strongly that women have to develop a language of their own, for every other language is misogynist."[2] At least, the stories collected in this volume allow a variety of women we may never have encountered before— such as a housewife from rural Majorca—to express themselves and to be heard. It is worth noting the exception of "Mon Semblable, Mon Frère," told from a man's point of view.

This collection is representative of the wit and irony that permeate Riera's later works. "A Matter of Self-Esteem" (1987) achieves a culmination of elements she had previously experimented with: first person, lyricism, sensuous language, baroque sentences. The plot unfolds in the sometimes desultory but always polished writing of Angela, a novelist in her late forties who constantly questions the basis of her reality, her motives, and the motives of those around her. The entire story consists of a letter written to her friend Ingrid that tells a tale of love and loss, hope and disillusionment, self-acceptance and narcissism. Finally succumbing to Ingrid's pleas, Angela writes, explaining why she has failed to contact her for more than a year. Her account of this disturbing period is characteristically humorous and poignant. The reader follows her sexual rediscovery, her recapture of self-confidence, and her encounter and subsequent loss of romantic love at a mature age.

Interestingly enough, her adventure begins at a literary conference, where Angela voices her opinion that literature has shunned the topic of eroticism in the mature woman. In her own text she will, in fact, correct this situation by giving a detailed account of her experience.

In addition to being a stylistic achievement, "A Matter of Self-Esteem" also marks the development of Riera's ability to create character. Although Angela's point of view controls the entire narration, two additional characters stand out as individuals: Miguel, the author with whom Angela falls in love, and Ingrid, whom the reader knows only indirectly through references in Angela's letter. While Ingrid is self-assured, sexually liberated, and extroverted—capable of dedicating a book "to the men and women of [my] life . . . in order of appearance"—Angela is introverted and hypersensitive, always referring to her embarrassment and reluctance. It is clear that Ingrid would never have fallen for Miguel.

Miguel, fraudulent both as a writer and as a lover, seduces and abandons Angela, and then uses their brief affair as material for his next novel. Not only does he mistreat Angela as a woman, he also strives to destroy her as an author. Miguel's seductive power works at the service of his narcissism, as the title of the story suggests. It is, however, an ambiguous title: It refers both to Miguel's excessive self-love and to Angela's lack of it. Once she realizes that Miguel has manipulated her for his own selfish purposes, Angela's self-esteem is very much at stake and in need of compensation. She will seek revenge, but unlike the heroines of Golden Age drama, who usually recover their lost honor by marrying their seducers, Angela avenges herself on the intellectual level.

Miguel's novel, appropriately titled *The Swan's Song*, provides an implicit subtext to Angela's letter, for, having stolen the idea from her, he too writes about a mature heroine in love; only in his version she is ridiculed.

In "A Matter of Self-Esteem" Riera also refines her subject matter. While her body of work reflects the varied nature of women and women's experience, here she focuses on a specific issue: an older woman's sexual identity crisis. Riera explores it without following a prescriptive agenda and without allowing her artistry to suffer in the service of an ideology. Spanish society, history, and literature are all called into question and subjected to Riera's personal brand of revisionism: Social commentary is present, but only when it directly relates to the plot, through the eyes of the narrator, who is sometimes prudish and other times quite frank. These shifts are not a result of any weakness, but rather of the insight that women are neither Mary nor Eve, but often an uneasy combination of the two. Although Ingrid's casual approach to sex fits the feminist ideal more closely, Riera doesn't necessarily take her side; she treats the vulnerable, romantic Angela with respect, implying that her attitudes about love and sex also deserve a place.

Introduction

There is thematic unity among these stories, and their two main subjects are interrelated: writers and love and, often, writers *in* love. In some cases, the writer-lover intellectually preys upon the other: Miguel in "A Matter," or the homosexual Rafel in "*Mon Semblable*." Both antiheroes have fraudulent talents; Miguel draws his historical information from the *Michelin* guides and his fictional plot from Angela's ideas, while Rafel passes the translations of his poems done by his friend José Ignacio as his own work. Both achieve success in the literary establishment by usurping their partners' brainchild and both feel their own inadequacies and a certain amount of guilt. Variations of the theme of the mirror, so dear to Riera, recur in these two tales of insecure identities. The narrator of "A Matter" believes that "it is, finally, in the mirror of the flesh that lovers recognize themselves, transgress the limits of the skin, and become one." Miguel is nothing but his writing, and his writing is a fake. His mirror is defective and can only reflect his own image, the only hero in his repertoire. On the other hand, Rafel—who titles his last book *The Mirrors*—and the writer-painter José Ignacio can't tell their images apart on the canvas, as they can't distinguish their life experiences and, ultimately, their poems.

More humorous versions of the fraudulent author are the media conscious Delmira Alonso Samblancat of "Report" (Informe), the gossip columnist of "Surprise at Sri Lanka," and the transsexual Juan/Juanita Chamorro of "The Seductive Genius" (La seducció del geni), who, lacking the novelistic gift himself, hopes to marry a famous writer in order to enjoy the creative process vicariously. In "Against Love in Company," Coral, whose seventy-year-old husband fails to satisfy her sexually, dismisses her own erotic poetry as "nothing but a fraud, pure and simple." Even Bernat, the chef of "Recipe Book," may be considered a dishonest author, in the sense that his collected recipes, to be published posthumously, are not what they seem to be.

As for Carme Riera's style, suffice it to say that it is unabashedly literary. She delights in convoluted sentences, elaborate metaphors, and sensuous descriptions, displaying her erudition in references to other writers, artists, even scientists. In her universe, imaginary characters interact with real figures of the contemporary literary world, thus breaking the conventional barrier between reality and fiction.

Intertextuality is also a common device. These stories often engage in dialogues with other novels, such as Leopoldo Alas's *La Regenta*, films, such as Luchino Visconti's *Senso*, poems, or even songs. Furthermore, the influence of the baroque discourse of the Spanish Golden Age—Riera's area of academic expertise—is apparent in the poetic language and intricate sentence patterns found in "A Matter of Self-Esteem." On another occasion we detect a reference to the sixteenth-century classic *Lazarillo de Tormes* in the phrase "the peak of good fortune" ("Surprise at Sri Lanka"). In sum, for Carme Riera the literary permeates everything, and the world cannot exist independently from literature.

The narrator of "A Matter of Self-Esteem" declares that "all writing is a love letter." Not long ago, Riera said "I write because I can't help it. I also write to seduce the reader."[3] There is no question of the sincerity or accuracy of these statements. Seduction and writing, writing and love, are all inextricable from each other. And when Riera writes, her tone is suggestive and insinuating, the rhythm of her prose hypnotic, and every sentence an imperceptible wink at the reader, a subtle invitation to follow the narrator through the labyrinth of the narrative. Miguel seduces Angela with smooth talk, but isn't Angela, in turn, seducing us, as she slowly and deliberately weaves her web? Isn't she, underneath her shyness and inhibitions and seemingly low self-esteem, another siren with an alluring song? As Akiko Tsuchiya states, "As a writer, Angela is intellectually aware that all narration is a form of erotic seduction."[4] So is Carme Riera who, through her narrator's voice, wants to seduce the reader; but, unlike the fraudulent writers in her stories, she will not cheat. The reader will be well advised not to resist.

ROSER CAMINALS-HEATH
HOLLY CASHMAN

NOTES

1.   Kathleen McNerney, *On Our Own Behalf: Women's Tales from Catalonia* (Lincoln: University of Nebraska Press, 1988), 2.

2.   Ibid., 13–14

3.   "Carme Riera." *Catalan Writing* 13 (May 1994), 61–64.

4.   Akiko Tsuchiya, "The Paradox of Narrative Seduction in Carme Riera's *Cuestión de amor propio.*" *Hispania* 75.2 (1992), 283.

*A Matter
of Self-Esteem
and Other Stories*

A Matter of Self-Esteem

Vallvidrera,[1] October 23, 1986

DEAREST INGRID: You are right. I accept your furious ultimatum. You never want to hear from me again if I don't answer your letter right away, explaining in detail what has kept me silent for so long. As you can see, I'm responding immediately—your letter came the day before yesterday—and I begin by asking for forgiveness. One year, I know, is too long an interval to claim the right to silence when you have given me no reason to do so. Quite the contrary. Believe me when I tell you that I have reread your letters often. On many occasions I have answered them, mentally, from the most unthinkable places; sometimes with the hope that despite the thousands of miles that separate us, you, who know me so well, would realize that my obsessive and almost always redundant monologues were meant to give you, and only you, proof of my existence and, especially, of my friendship.

A little over a week ago, I was about to take a plane just to come and spend a few hours with you, unburden my conscience, and then return selfishly comforted with your advice. The light of a fleeting autumn dusk, the opaline shade of four in the afternoon that you dislike so much, would have been far more conducive to exchanging confidences than this conventional mode of communication which, even with the help of the pen you gave me, I still mistrust, being as it is much less personal than the voice, for it steals away all the intricacies I would like to convey with words. The telephone, however, is even more uncomfortable: if it rings at a bad time it may be counterproductive, forcing me to be brief, to compress hurriedly in a few minutes what, surely, will take me hours to explain.

I promise you that I will try to make my handwriting as clear as possible. Don't think it's easy, accustomed as I am to writing only for myself or for my typist, who knows my longhand well. Moreover, this scribbling may be but a ruse of my inescapable coyness—you already know about my boundless timidity—to draw an imaginary line of defense. I frequently hide behind the mask of my dreadful handwriting. In this way I make those people with whom I correspond—those few I actually care about—spend more time deciphering my messages. With you, however, the opposite has been true: I have always tried to be direct and explicit, even in my handwriting. If some of its features remain difficult to understand, don't attribute it to this professed weakness that I have never displayed with you; blame rather the unconscious barriers that my reclusive temperament has built, striving to defer with inkblots the confidences that I want to share with you anyway, or allowing them to flow freely like the ink of this old fountain pen I so much like to use.

To this long list of excuses I should add the landscape as well; you already know how intensely landscapes influence my spirit. So different from yours, the scenery I contemplate doesn't help me find the right tone to communicate all I want without boring you to tears. Yes, Ingrid, I seek the perfect way to convey to you everything that has happened to me. I'm sure you have already guessed by now that one of the causes of my reticence has been precisely the fear of appearing before you fragile, helpless, full of prejudice and, above all, ridiculous.

How strange! In your last letter, in addition to firing a volley of insults at me for having kept you uninformed so long, you described your garden: "The light has the same copper tones as when you last visited; the fir trees we planted together have grown very tall; the linden trees are beginning to lose their leaves and only the holly remains in blossom. You don't know how reverently I watch these flowers that still endure. In no time the snow will cover everything; the winter will stretch its polar bear skin over the entire country and I, as I do every year, will pine for the southern greens, the southern flowers, and your southern light. The light that never comes from the North—as you, mimicking Maragall's critique of *The Intruder*,[2] humorously remind me whenever I complain about this—but rather from the South, where it sharpens the edges of things and presents them in absolute clarity."

Yes, my dearest Ingrid, that fiery southern light, at times like this, can be a disadvantage; not only because it draws us to open vistas, like outdoor cafes, making us falsely outgoing, but also because it crudely reveals our flaws, edges, bumps, without shame and with the utmost precision. This light makes us realize that objects have rough profiles, that vegetables have sinewy stems, and that everything, or almost everything, displays the aggressiveness of the knife, the incisive sharpness of the engraver, if not the terrible—yet beautiful—hardness of the diamond itself. And precisely because of this powerful light, the world that we see appears bristled, as if in continuous erection. I find much more appealing the shadows that envelop the northern lands, the diffused tones that surround objects and shorten distances. The smooth paleness of your foggy days is much more inviting and has a positive effect on me, although in truth it also fosters melancholy. No, Ingrid, I don't associate male divinities with the South, nor beneficent lunar goddesses with the North. Not at all. A character as misogynistic as Unamuno[3] related—successfully, as I now realize—the indifference the Spaniards have for memoirs and letters—confessional literature, as he called it—to their vehement temperament inclined to extreme notions; such notions, he suggested, were born perhaps of this furious Mediterranean light I loved so much when, a long time ago, I used to believe that summer was the ultimate season.

All of this may be the reason why I have begun this letter alluding to the difficulty of writing to you at this time of year, possibly because at my mature age my sensibility is closer to the slow rhythm and faint pulse of autumn. At the same time the luxuriant abundance of colors in the landscape—those reds that burn the branches of the trees, the nearly copper hue of the little bushes, the greens that give way to straw yellows and the scattered, voluptuous ocher of thousands of fallen leaves—touch me in a special way. The beauty of these colors is as changing as it is ephemeral. Here, fall is a much more fleeting season than in your country. Constrained by a summer that lingers like an unwelcome visitor — sometimes, like last year, until November—and a winter that arrives unexpectedly, conquering and implacable, like an army whose strategy consists in taking the enemy territory by surprise, the season barely has time to reveal itself. Perhaps my growing fondness for mortal things, my interest in all that fades and evaporates, has finally made fall my favorite season.

Furthermore, Gridi, the story that I'm trying to postpone with so many warnings and preambles began and ended on those days that, according to the calendar, belong to fall, although a cruel, lingering light seemed to extend the summer and the heat forced us to wear light clothes, almost like now.

I know very well, Ingrid, that I should avoid delay and stop beating around the bush. Before I get to the point, however, I must repeat once again what I have assured you of so many times: The only experiences that are worth living intensely, risking everything if necessary, are those that, thanks to their beauty and their power to fascinate us, we may transform into so fine a recollection that it can possibly thwart death.

Since I was a child, memory has been everything for me. I think that the power to summon it at any moment and, especially, at key moments, in order to scrutinize its darkest recesses, has drawn me, in part, to writing. Forgive me if I insist on this aspect of myself that you already know and dislike, but I want you to keep it fresh in your mind as you judge my behavior, if in fact I'm able to explain my actions with reasonable accuracy. Although I maintain an intimate relationship with words—literature is little more than words—when I rely on them, not to describe people's feelings, create characters, or construct imaginary situations, but rather to ponder over my own existence in the first person, I'm awkward, obtuse, and hardly able to find the word that fits appropriately with the content.

A Matter of Self-Esteem

What I write or say is a pale reflection of what I want to express. Now I have recovered the serenity I so much needed and can see it all with more detachment, with a certain irony and sufficient clarity to know that the paralyzing anguish of last year was due, above all, to a moral disease that drove me—I won't deny it—to calculate obsessively the ideal proportion of alcohol and barbiturates for a successful mix, or the distance required between the window and the pavement in order to achieve the desired end. Even now, however, when I'm almost cured of everything, I fear that words won't sit well with the sensations, feelings, and ideas that I want to describe to you and that they may ring false.

I know that you, Ingrid, are one of the few people in my emotional environment capable of understanding this fear. Our long friendship has given you the clues to it. Furthermore, you are used to expressing yourself in writing and are familiar with all these terrors. If you add to this the fact that while my illness lasted I was incapable of writing a single line, you'll understand even better the infinite pain it caused me. I imagine that if I had contracted it at eighteen, rather than at forty-eight, my system would have resisted better; or, if on various occasions I had become slightly infected, my organism would have developed a sort of vaccine, the necessary antibodies to combat the virus. But I wasn't so lucky. Perhaps my marriage, which failed beautifully—as Jaime likes to say when I sporadically see him—and some equally negative adolescent experiences produced in me a visceral rejection of any serious relationship. A strange instinct made me flee in time. I assumed that my devotion wouldn't be reciprocated and I saw myself as a fool, with nothing to look forward to except a pair of eyes that, quite possibly, wouldn't even look me in the face. This cowardice, or whatever you want to call it, has protected me against possible adventures and foreseeable suffering.

I remember very well that often on our long walks through the Aarhus Campus, you would reproach me for my timid attitude toward love. You advised me to adopt a much more open stance, to consider sex just another appetite, a necessity that must be satisfied in order to maintain physical and mental balance. For you, intimate contact with other bodies is enriching; pleasure is a way of making up for life's emptiness, as well as one of the most valid means of knowing reality. I, on the other hand, belong to the type of woman—an endangered species — who is incapable of entering someone's arms without being in love. And I would never have been able to dedicate a book "To the men and women of my life," as you did, adding a long list of names in, as you noted, the order of appearance.

I still keep among the commentaries on *Interior with Figures* the one you gave me in private, in a lovely letter: "Your novels," you wrote, "would greatly improve if you could resolve your sex life for yourself, instead of through the orgasms of your characters, if you could accept desire naturally and with no qualms.

A Matter of Self-Esteem

I would not give up any of my lovers, not even those whose faces and bodies I have forgotten. They have all made positive contributions to my life, they have enriched it . . ."

Perhaps the thousands of miles between us and this different light which, when one faces the Mediterranean, seems to invite a pagan blameless pleasure, have made us look at these issues in different ways and, contrary to what you'd expect, have weakened my interest in sex. Actually, what I'm looking for—the same thing that, I'm almost sure, most women of my generation are or were after—is tenderness: that feeling that restores us to the forever blue garden of childhood where any nightmare would disappear as if by magic, fleeing from the warm, sweet voice of the mother who cradled us. And yet, many of us, especially the most combative who passed for the more intelligent, became embarrassed by this tendency toward tenderness, because it seemed to us to be a feminine weakness. We preferred to show ourselves before others, particularly before men, as cold, strong, and self-sufficient. And since I am already on my knees and in front of the confessional screen—that huge vertical colander that filters blame and penitence—I'll add that one thing I've wanted all my life is for someone to hold me and call me "my little one," even if my feminist principles were seriously compromised and my commitment weakened in having to admit that I not only accepted, but rather wanted to be diminished, objectified, and almost degraded.

You can believe me if I tell you that from my break-up with Jaime seven years ago till this past November I hadn't slept with anyone. This makes me feel neither bad nor frustrated, not at all. However, the warmth of another body in bed, the contact, albeit furtive, of another skin while going to sleep, these were painful deprivations. More difficult still was having to do without not so much the company as the complicity, the shared defense against the ingratitude and pettiness of life, which is easier to bear for two than it is for one. Even now, after rediscovering the powerful call of desire, the dark bond that in the instant of total abandon, of absolute surrender, we establish with eternity and that lifts us momentarily to the plenitude of the gods, I continue to believe this. If I were by your side, in the living room of your house in Stjaer, you'd reply instantly that these gratifying feelings are generated only by pleasure, which has to do with biochemistry: that the rest is nothing but frills that conventional people like me use to disguise human animality. Maybe you're right and it all boils down to a matter of hormones, to the correct functioning of a series of glands, invisible stimuli, an erotic dance of courtship flowing imperceptibly. However, I have never surrendered my flesh without the assurance that other less biological, more animistic and spiritual aspects of myself—I know you detest these words, but I have no others—were also part of this fusion and of this splendid confusion. Again, this time I wasn't aware of any chemical stimulant;

but I did notice the instant in which the divine archer fired his golden arrows and my missing half, after the catastrophe that condemned us to a very long separation, rejoined my self. The world—this is a platitude, I know, but so it happened—regained all its meaning, a primeval, unusual, harmonious meaning. And the more or less fortunate phrases I articulated at interviews or round table discussions ("all writing is a love letter," "I write to be loved," "the yearning for self-perpetuation spurs us to love as well as to create," "text is nothing but an erotic pretext") had finally reached the only destination I cared about—the "other" that would justify my existence from then on and for whom, unbeknownst to me, I had kept in my loneliness a spiritual, if not physical, virginity; for I had never felt a greater interest, a more complete absorption in anyone. Our affinities, which might have come from comparable experiences and upbringings—when I was born, he was five—seemed to me proof of our fatal predestination. Not only did we favor the same authors, painters, and composers, but even liked the same books, paintings, and symphonies; particular passages, brush strokes, and beats would touch us in the same way. Our tastes in more ordinary matters—food, decor, or clothing—were also similar and we shared a fascination for the misty coasts of Northern Europe, where we hoped to travel as soon as possible. If our plans had materialized you'd have met him, for my insistence on visiting your country had a lot to do with my desire to bring the two of you into contact; or, since you already were in contact even though you didn't know it, I wanted for you to give me your blessing and feel proud of me, just this once, because I had finally set literature aside and chosen life.

I so much wanted to surprise you that I decided not to tell you about the affair in writing, but to show up unexpectedly with my lover, like you did that summer in Tossa when you came with Andreas and, with a charming shamelessness, asked Jaime and me, "What do you think, does he suit me?" I was sure you'd love Miguel and think he suited me marvelously. Right away I pictured the three of us next to the chimney in the living room talking and talking, engaged in endless conversation. And it's possible that this endless conversation —of course, just between you two—will take place very soon, as Miguel—his name is very appropriate, you'll see—is going to Scandinavia in a month. But I don't want to get ahead of myself.

I think that in my last letter, over a year ago, I said I was going to take part in a writers conference in Valencia. The truth is that I wasn't looking forward to it. If I attended it's because I usually reserve part of the year for these duties in order to satisfy my publisher, who's conscious of the high visibility such events provide; otherwise, I felt no personal inclination to go. With few exceptions, I'm not interested in writers, although as a child I worshipped them with reverence. Not only did I collect their autographs in an impecca-

A Matter of Self-Esteem

ble notebook, but I also corresponded with many of them; worse yet, I secretly hoped to marry a promising, undiscovered figure whom I would help succeed. Thanks to my encouragement, glory and fortune would be his. He would revitalize the avant garde and then be inducted into the Academy. The fact that Jaime, as a good economist turned banker, cared only about bounced checks, made things difficult for me and, in a way, may have motivated me to take up writing. From then on, particularly after the favorable reception of my second book, my fascination with writers and their creative powers almost disappeared. I don't maintain a terribly good relationship with myself—in fact, I hardly value my capacities—although perhaps what happened in Valencia partly contradicts this statement. My propensity for amazement at the skill of a word charmer, which I thought I'd forgotten, revived when Miguel spoke in the Golden Salon of the old Valencia Exchange. The wizard of my adolescence— the magician who could release a flock of doves from a top hat, tie and untie handkerchiefs in the blink of an eye and, in the grand finale, cut off the head of his assistant only to reattach it in a flash with the help of a few words—was before me once more, happily acknowledging the audience's applause. The next day it happened again. His presentation was the most brilliant, insightful, and polished of those I heard. Although I knew his work well enough—no wonder, as he was, and is, one of the most critically acclaimed of all the popular writers—and I admired the arrogant wit of his public statements, I had never met him. Nor did I ask to be introduced this time. With a self-assurance that surprised me, I decided to use every means available to make him interested in me, without go-betweens. Gradually my curiosity was developing into fascination.

In that afternoon's session, the discussion focused on the influence of nineteenth-century literature on the contemporary novel, particularly on the role of *La Regenta*.[4] Talk dragged on without incident till Miguel's turn came. With the skill of an accomplished swordsman, he brandished the argument that, for the first time in Spanish narrative, sexuality had been taken into consideration. No other realist novel had put such an emphasis on eroticism, and, because of this triumph of matter over spirit, we should credit Clarín[5] with the breath of fresh European air that naturalism finally brought to Spain. Ana Ozores' problem, the problem of all the Ana Ozoreses, of the time, was not just that of a maladjusted personality, but rather of an unsatisfied libido.

Having listened to him, I reached the conclusion that the best way to catch his attention would be to contradict him. With the effort it takes a consumptive to suppress a coughing fit, I raised my hand to ask for the floor and refuted Miguel's argument. To my way of understanding, Ana Ozores' frustration came entirely from her loveless childhood, which in part predetermined her character; for this reason, the adventure with Germán in the little boat at Trébol is crucial. What happened that night between the children is one of Ana Ozores' few pleasant memories. For the first time someone tells her a story and, also for the first time, someone covers her up before going to sleep by her side. Up to that point, Ana had had no way to put herself to sleep other than by telling herself bedtime stories, searching her own imagination to keep herself company. These longings, far more than the pursuit of sexual satisfaction, dominate the life of the Regent's wife. She gave herself to the unworthy Mesía, trusting that every night, after loving her and tucking her in, he would tell her a new story.

My interruption surprised him. We debated before our expectant fellow writers, who must have found my timid appearance at odds with the incisive tone of my arguments. He concluded by intimating slyly that my views indicated a marked feminine tendency—and he said this with an emphatic complicity—to restrain powerful sexual drives. I replied, to some faint applause, that only women are in the position to decide if we feel, not like gods, but like goddesses—I emphasized—when orgasm triumphs or if what we feel is simply a matter of tenderness.

In the evening, as soon as I walked into the dining room of the hotel I knew that my fate was sealed. Not only had he saved me a seat at the table, but he went out of his way to compliment me. He had never met a colleague so compatible with him. I was the most interesting person at the conference, the first woman to dot her i's and cross her t's in a public debate; moreover, he had read my work. . . . Never had I felt so sure of myself or been as determined to seize an opportunity. Instead of hiding the attraction he aroused in me, I chose to reveal it openly and naturally.

We didn't have coffee with everyone else. We drank it alone on a surreal veranda in Malvarrosa. It was a musical, voraciously sensuous evening, perfectly suited for bearing one's soul from the waist down, but we both avoided confidences and restricted our conversation to professional topics. We spoke about Clarín and Galdós,[6] about literature and ethics, and, I don't know why, we discussed the reluctance that novelists have shown throughout history to make women over thirty their love-sick heroines.

"Literary conventions assume that nothing happens after maturity that merits being written about." But Miguel replied that a man of almost fifty is the protagonist of the best Spanish novel. "In any case, your example is the exception to the rule. Alonso Quijano,[7] in making himself a knight errant, changed his name, his status, his way of life and, even if Cervantes doesn't say so, he believed himself to be young, as the context makes clear. You must agree that older characters, especially women, are not very common in the novel."

"But what about *Doña Perfecta* or *Misericordia?*"[8]

"Doña Perfecta demonstrates my point precisely.

She is the epitome of the conservatism and stupidity that mature female characters usually embody. Notice how, even as minor characters—mothers, aunts, grand-mothers or mothers-in-law—old women are generally grumpy, hypocritical, sour, miserly creatures who resent the triumph of youth."

Miguel listened to me as eagerly as a defendant about to hear the verdict, as if his life hinged on my words. I added flirtatiously, "Love is women's opium, of course, but only for the young ones. " He politely disagreed, bringing up a trivial point while he raised my hand to his lips.

Throughout the five days of the conference we were hardly apart. I could still retrace that sentimental journey across the map of Valencia, which had noth-ing to do with predictable itineraries full of baroque surprises and disguised gothic windows, but rather with avenues crazed with traffic and drab ugliness, which I crossed all too frequently just to feel the gentle touch of his hand on my elbow. I could also identify the bars we frequented in the old city, whose benches allowed us to sit very close, our thighs and legs touching promiscu-ously while we talked a bit about the divine and a lot about the human. At one of those grimy tables, already on the verge of daybreak, when the inconsiderate dawn was beginning to scratch the window panes at the hour of overpowering sleepiness and worn-out glasses, for the first time his fingers casually traced hieroglyphics on my hands, cryptic marks on my arms, and lingered with the deliberation of a sculptor on my face and hair. And this hour of morning's first light that I had always hated, perhaps because through my early years at boarding school it coincided with the alarm clock's ring and a cold shower and, in my adolescence, with the ends of those pleasant parties, suddenly became the sweetest in my memory, my favorite.

During the day, when we joined the others at those dreadful literary sessions the conference director forced upon us with a Prussian discipline that he called simply academic, I felt that Miguel and I shared an intense and complex secret life that isolated us from the rest. Settled in the last rows of the lecture room we whispered remarks unrelated to what, in theory, we were listening to, or exchanged messages that started out as silly notes and ended up as "charter documents of our love," in his terminology, priceless records for our future biographers that he was determined to keep himself. We even initiated a dual narrative, swapping paragraphs as if we were projecting ourselves in a game of mirrors.

> *Wise woman, give me a crumb*
> *of thy bread, to take away the bitterness*
> *of all food, for I have no appetite*
> *except that which is satiated with love* [9]

A Matter of Self-Esteem

Ausias March prescribed the adequate recipe and the September moon reflected on the sea delivered the rest. Even though no hoarse music played and no wind moaned against the sails, nor were we in the stern of any ship, his voice must have sounded like that of a pirate in my ear, and his words even more daring.[10]

"These borrowed lines express better than my poor words everything you make me feel."

And meanwhile, like a ridiculous, blinded butterfly, I burned in the fiery light of his eyes. His voice, especially made up for the occasion, murmured, velvety, in my ear, "My desire for you is greater than the ocean, more profound than the abyss. I'll love you as long as I live because no one has ever reached so far inside me, penetrated me so deeply. Because of this, I want to be better for you day after day . . . "

Ingrid, you recognize these as trivial phrases, besides being bombastic and even corny; they reeked of sweaty seminarian and parochial rhetoric. However, for me they were heavenly music maybe because I had been waiting for them, not for a week, but for months or years, perhaps for my entire life, and because they came from somebody who could not be interested in me as a writer, in order to thrive in my shadow, nor, given my age, as a trophy worthy of display. Nor would my reclusion, my contempt for politics, my lack of ambition in this respect lure an opportunist. More likely, I was the one who might take advantage of Miguel's position in the cultural milieu now that, exactly a month before our meeting, he had been appointed Director of the Foundation for Cultural Progress, doubtless one of the most important organizations in the country.

Bear with me again, dear Ingrid. Only if you stay by me will I be able to withstand the assaults of my memory that so obsessively, especially this past winter, brought back to me the tracks of our rhythmic steps on the damp sand and the intertwined shadows of our bodies next to a deep sea and a happy beach. I didn't resort to Ausias March or Pere Serafí or Jordi de Sant Jordi.[11] I didn't pretend to match text and context. I used a verse from Salinas[12] that had often pounded in my brain and that, perhaps, I had always reserved for a similar occasion before it perfectly summed up my emotional state; moreover, it was a borrowed citation that allowed me to continue in the literary vein he had established:

> *Fear of you.*
> *To love you is the highest risk.*

I was afraid, Ingrid, of everything or nearly everything. Afraid of my age, of my body—not exactly in its prime—that exhibited, even in its most intimate folds and hidden recesses, the clumsy caress of time, and whose most vulnerable zones the years had plentifully ravaged. And, above all, I was afraid of my face, which love's abandonment would leave without make-up to conceal the frown of the mouth, now permanently between parentheses, without the aid of protective shadows that mask bags, rings, and wrinkles, or the corrective pen that erases the worst crow's-feet. Furthermore, I feared surrendering myself too quickly.

My plane was leaving at dawn. We had four hours left, hardly enough time for the "process" to take place according to the ritual I wanted to establish. Perhaps to compensate for my physical decline, I wanted to appear more experienced than I was and offer him the possibility of exploring voluptuous territories together, lingering in their paths so that the prelude would be as long as the pleasure intense. For this reason, I asked him at the door of my room to put it off until a future rendezvous, which would be definitive.

I don't think I have to tell you I didn't sleep a wink. I was allergic to the touch of the sheets; I needed the contact of his body, his languid hands around my waist, the dangerous fire of his lips burning on my mouth and his miraculous voice in my ear, even if he kept talking about his work or his family, about his bright children or his little wife, with whom he of course maintained a routine relationship of coexistence. I was on the verge of calling his room and asking him to come, or moving to his and curling up by his side without further ado, greedy for his protection. If I didn't do it, it was because I would never have forgiven myself for a failure due to haste, as if, out of negligence, I tipped an inkwell onto a priceless first edition.

If you're still reading this, Ingrid, if you haven't yet died of boredom, I'm sure you'll be furious. I'm not surprised. At this point I'm furious too, because I'm conscious of my stupidity. How ridiculous I must have seemed to him, with my efforts to offer him a doctored postcard—full moon, calm sea, and a declaration of love—not realizing that he must have it already in his collection; carrying myself as if I was fifteen, only not in 1925 but in the last century, at the peak of the Romantic fever, while Günderrode[13] killed herself and Schubert composed his most sclerotic pieces. For now you'll have to control your displeasure, my dear, and defer your reprimand, because I made even greater mistakes. Later you may scold me all that you want. Shout at me, as you usually do. I'm ready to accept whatever punishment you may prescribe, particularly if you do me the favor I'm trying to ask in this letter, whose length might compensate for my prolonged silence. So that you will have the full story, I'll endeavor to focus my memory not on recollections, but on facts. I'm afraid that after so much handling, after going over them so many times during this year, they may reflect inadequately those experiences and restore them to me blurred by the haze of time.

Precisely one of the most painful consequences of this story has been the impossibility of recalling any of its positive aspects. Through the first months of my illness I tried to remember the trembling of my hand between his, which, like a cradle and a cup, seemed made to the specifications of my exhaustion and my thirst; or the taste of his kisses, in which I forgot all those that didn't come from his lips. But the hostile memory didn't bring me any gratifying sensation, quite the contrary. More discouraging yet was the impossibility of recapturing the slightest pleasure. My tongue, cold and lifeless in my mouth, was unable to recover even the skeleton of a kiss.

The corpse of an orchid, perfectly exquisite in its little plastic casket, waited for me upon my return to Valencia. An unsigned card dated that same morning read "I love you now and always." Other orchids with similar notes, sent from cities to which Miguel frequently traveled on business, followed during those weeks. Orchids alternated with letters written on elegant paper embossed with his initials: "I die to think of the moment when I'll see you again, for I love you more than I ever imagined I could" (9/25/85); "I ask myself how I have lived so long without you and I can only answer that I wasn't really alive" (9/30/85); "I've returned to the wet dreams of my adolescence. Do you understand what this means? . . . an incredible desire for you" (9/23/85); "I'm giving serious thought to initiating the divorce proceedings. I want to marry you" (10/5/85); "I strolled through the city with your absence on my arm, my dearest" (7/10/85); "The days last forever. All I want is for them to fly: barely a week before I see you, before I love you. I don't know if I can take it" (10/17/85); "No one will be able to separate us, my love, Angela, my angel, because I am definitively yours" (10/20/85); "Listen carefully, I will never leave you, NEVER. No matter if you reject me, withdraw, move away, I'll go after you" (10/23/85).

I think I could also repeat verbatim our phone conversations, splashed with affectionate topics, ad hoc loving phrases, warm and never-ending good-byes, almost imitating those operatic farewells in which the *addio* extracts a deep *do* from the tenor or even a duet with the soprano. The telephone, even more than the mail, was our ally. It could ring at the most unlikely times, simply "to hear you, that's all"; to consult me on some triviality—the right color tie to match a suit (the president would be at the reception); to ask for advice on the subject of a lecture or to read me the most recent article he had written. The telephone confirmed my reputation for tardiness; I became accustomed to the taste of cold food and to interrupted sleep, and I didn't care. The telephone, that telephone I had always hated, became a sort of umbilical cord that kept us constantly united. Sweetly shackled to my ears—an imprisonment, I hoped, for life—the telephone became as indispensable to me as Melibea's belt to Calixto[14] and I compared it to "that hair interlaced" with every joy and garland. . . . My God, what stupid hyperboles! The terrible thing is, Gridi, that at the time they didn't seem so. On the contrary. And, for the first time, the literary examples I made use of revealed to me their entire meaning. On the other hand, now that I can look ironically upon my behavior, I have reached the conclusion that telephone company executives understand perfectly the influence their gimmick has on love affairs. And these extra services, like telephone erotica or even the hope line, should find their most faithful customers among those with ears sensitive to a certain type of caressing voice (I imagine you now looking for some biological explanation).

Almost a month after we had met in Valencia, Miguel informed me that we could spend a weekend together. He had made arrangements to be with me for three peaceful days, loving each other unhurriedly, as I had requested, listening to our intimate friend Wolfgang Amadeus, and rediscovering together the pious naiveté of Romanesque tableaux and the contours of Gaudí.[15] All of my fears disappeared. I was in great shape. Not as plain as usual, I might have almost described myself as attractive, and that gave me strength. I knew that anything touched by love is beautifully transformed and that desire bestows a shining halo upon those who claim it as an ally. I felt in a state of grace and took pleasure in personally attending to the most insignificant but indispensable details: his favorite brand of malt whisky, the least emaciated orchids I could find, and our own favorite Mozart selections—the quintet for clarinet and the Piano Concerto no. 21. I lit the fireplace, even though it wasn't cold yet. I yearned to make love by the fire, hoping perhaps to summon the spirits of summer and, at the same time, to burn, if only symbolically, our past lives, like Edith Piaf: "*Balayé pour toujours ça commence avec toi.*"[16]

Through the windows, the usual trees in the garden retained their green summer hue. On the glass panes the dancing flames glowed, outlining the embers with iridescence. As if reflected on a delicate plate, a single image reconciled the calm deliberation of the leaves and the rapid disintegration of the logs. An unrepeatable instant of brief contrast, tarnished by the mere act of describing it. Absolute perfection in the exhausted silence of an endless death.

I don't wish to appear even more ridiculous, but I assure you that up until then my skin had not yet felt the glory of touch: the nearly imperceptible softness of a butterfly's wings, the fluidity of petals and music, the slow intrusion of daggers.

Through that night I wanted to be Faust so that I could sell my soul to Mephistopheles in exchange for being transformed into Margaret.[17] Suddenly, nothing that had interested me before mattered; neither my thirst for knowledge nor my creative abilities: only to be young and to regain the beauty and innocence that captivated Faust. I hardly remembered the disastrous end—imagine the extent of my folly. I think that, in a way, my dreams came true and, what is more, quite soon.

Our story, or rather, my story, lasted exactly a month and a half, and the breakup came inexplicably after our first and last night of love. I still don't know precisely why, although I've taken all the time in the world to analyze the possible causes, to which I can now add one more that may be definitive. Miguel left my house on a Friday almost at daybreak in early November. He had to give up the weekend for a meeting as unforeseen as urgent, thus ruining a good part of our plans. On a Thursday we had shared a Saturday night fever, as if we had been accidental lovers rather than literary heroes. That's why neither the obsessively conjugated verb to love, nor words like eternity, heaven, or ecstasy seemed inappropriate. Quite the opposite. I repeated them tirelessly in my vows to him.

He didn't want me to see him off at the airport. The idea of leaving me in the ramshackle hangar all alone horrified him. He asked me to stay in bed, so that his caresses might linger on my body, and suggested that I listen once again to the Brahms concerto "that was playing the moment we were transported to heaven." At the last minute, after the kind of hurried kiss he might have given me at the train station, Miguel turned around in the doorway to tell me, "How could I have ever guessed that this heart of glass possessed so much passion?"

The now customary orchid arrived by mid-morning from the airport with the laconic message: "Thank you very much." But that night he didn't call, nor did he the following day or the next. Nor did he write or send any more flowers. He simply evaporated, disappeared as if the earth had swallowed him. Our story— my story, excuse me—was left interrupted in this way, suddenly, when he shut my door behind him with a powerful slam that apparently struck him with the deepest amnesia.

I sat vigilant by the phone for the first forty-eight hours. My trust in him was so absolute that I thought only an accident or a sudden illness could explain his silence. I didn't dare call his house—he had insisted that, for the time being, we keep up appearances—or get in touch with his obnoxious, perfect secretary, who, I know, hated me. I did, however, contact mutual friends, who I assumed would be aware of whatever mishap had befallen him, to no avail. Finally, after four days, the weekend passed, I ate crow and called his house. A young cleaning girl courteously told me that the man of the house was not there. Then I called his office.

The efficient, perfect secretary assured me that he had gone abroad and would not return for ten days. I didn't know what to think. I couldn't understand why he hadn't mentioned a word about this trip, although at times I imagined that it involved some urgent, last minute business, and so I kept waiting for any news. Six days after those calls, I came across a picture of Miguel while absent-mindedly flipping through an issue of *Breakthrough 36* in my dentist's waiting room. He was radiant, with a glass in one hand and in the other the waist of an exuberant woman with an available look leaning slightly to the right against a blurry blue background. The photo's caption was explicit enough: "Writers have fun too." The brief news article explained that the well-known businessman Amet Barrut al Xatu, future patron of a Hispano-Arabic foundation, had invited a group of intellectuals, artists, and dignitaries on a Mediterranean cruise in order to compare points of view.

I never imagined that sorrow could take such an obsessive, even melodramatic form. Although it still wasn't cold, I spent hours by the fireplace staring into the fire in a nearly catatonic state. The flames, through a teary veil, displayed a strange phosphorescence, a new trembling. I counted the days until his return because I assumed that then, finally, he would show signs of life. Sometimes when I was calmer I summoned his presence by reading his letters, which I memorized, and rereading his novels. Precisely in those days, I realized that the worldly artistic references he so adeptly dropped seemed to appear in the paragraphs of the *Michelin* guides alarmingly often; that the baroque concertos his characters were so fond of were mistakenly attributed; and that his male protagonists, especially those who find success, had a bombastic, almost pompous attitude toward life that suddenly seemed incoherent and grotesque to me. I read his books with new eyes and discovered an infinity of details on pedantic display that I recognized as a string of falsehoods. I know that the poet is a pretender, that he even has an obligation to be so and that it is through this pretense that he proves most sincere. Never is an

actor more convincing than when he indeed "acts,"
plays a character different from himself, gets inside of
someone he isn't. Never is he so truthful as when he
lies. However, the world Miguel created in his novels
seemed to me made of cardboard, lacking moral cohe-
sion or a consistent point of view to give it true identity.
On the other hand, I again admired his ability to keep
the reader's interest until the end, creating a great
anticipation in the last chapters by intensifying the
action. And, as always, his skillful handling of a wide
linguistic range seduced me. It was precisely this
quality in his work that made me realize that maybe
our highly literary relationship, based as it was on
words, had ended as it did, suddenly, because he had
nothing left to say to me. He had tried different for-
mulas, used almost all of the resources within his
power, exhausted his verbal capacity. He had written
our relationship; he hadn't lived it. Perhaps he and I
were nothing but a jumble of words that now, all of a
sudden, collapsed with pain, sound, and fury, threat-
ening to crush us; or maybe we weren't even that, but
rather some minor entity: a sticky meringue pie beginning to ferment. That morning, when he shut the front
door, Miguel left behind, still wrapped in cellophane
and decorated with a big pink ribbon, protected but
already contaminated, the words with which I would
try hopelessly to make sense of our relationship and,
above all, of this unexpected end. Perhaps our
story—and now I have reason to believe this—was

nothing but a writing test, a laboratory experiment.

But to this interpretation I would add another, although subconsciously I wanted to reject it because it's much more painful: First of all, he equated me with one of those insipid heroines of the most dreadful soap operas, seduced and abandoned for being stupid and lacking a shred of insight; second, he made me into a simple object, a plate, a glass, a paper napkin, which, having been used once, is tossed into the garbage. However, I thought more highly of myself. Quite in keeping with my visceral refusal to let anyone eat out of my hand, I would have compared myself to good Sèvres china that one uses with the utmost care only on holidays. Of course, today Sèvres china is a bit antiquated. . . .

Perhaps Miguel, who's more at home in the world of fiction than in real life, couldn't forget that in Hispanic literature—maybe in the North this is different, you know: "*C'est toujours du nord que nous viens la lumière*"[18]—a woman pushing fifty has no right to love, much less to physical desire. To dare to love, to allow yourself to be loved, to wish to be loved with the same, if not greater, intensity than at twenty, is evidently dangerous and seems obscene. If an autumnal woman wants adventure, if she refuses to retire from life, both literature and cinema usually depict her paying a gigolo, that's to say, degraded. I wonder if he was terrified of my impassioned surrender, my insatiable need for love, my boundless desire, my capacity of transgressing this strict law that apparently forbids me, at my age, any erotic whim. Maybe it seemed so improper or even evil that it sent him away, never to return.

Like the archangel he's meant to honor—I already told you his name fits his personality well—Miguel also cut down my possibilities of rebellion and threw me, or at least tried to throw me, into Hell as his namesake did with Lucifer. No, this conclusion isn't so crazy, Ingrid, although he possibly wasn't able to admit it to himself.

However, I expected a different explanation from him. I assumed that he would argue that he didn't want to abandon his family or damage his public image, of which he was so conscious. Consequently, his justification would probably be limited to a simple enumeration of platitudes, punctuated with the usual fireworks: "You'll always be something special to me," or "I'll never forget you as long as I live." Ingrid, I confess that I was bracing myself to hear them upon his return, for I had learned that his cruise ended in Barcelona. I prepared an appropriate retort, painstakingly calculating a viable strategy to disarm and possibly captivate him. But this confrontation never took place. He passed through without even calling. I suppose he hurriedly flew to Madrid and plunged into the whirlpool of his work and his family life as if I had never been his, as if we had never met and that month and a half of letters, flowers, and phone calls had never existed. After pursuing him for many days through phone lines and extensions, I finally reached him.

"I can't believe it's you! How wonderful! How are you! Tell me, what can I do for you?"

I never expected such professional cordiality. I didn't hang up, although this unknown voice, made of concrete and plaster, seemed to belong to a completely different person. "I want to see you. We have to talk."

"Of course, I agree, I'd love to. We have so much to talk about! These days have been exhausting but worthwhile. You don't know how much I've done. By the way, there's a million things that might interest you. We need consultants. But tell me, where are you?"

"At home, in Barcelona."

"Oh! In Barcelona? I have to find some free time . . . so we can talk at length. If only I didn't have so much work. . . . I'm afraid I won't be able to get to Barcelona for a couple of months."

"Don't worry. I have to go to Madrid."

"To Madrid? Great! I've discovered an exquisite restaurant with a wonderful atmosphere and impeccable service. Will you do me the honor of joining me? You'll love it, you'll see. Besides, they have the good taste to play Mozart. . . . Angela, Angela. I want to talk to you so badly! Yes, yes, I want your input; there are so many things to talk over with you. Your opinions have always been so useful. . . . These days I haven't had a moment to myself, not even to listen to music. Oh! I envy your peaceful life. But it was worth it. Things at the Foundation are definitely on the right track. But enough of all that, don't you have anything to say? How are you? What are you doing? When are you coming?"

"Monday."

"Monday, Monday . . . let me check my calendar. Let's see . . . . What a shame! I have a horrible bankers' dinner. Do you remember I told you about these funds they were about to approve for us?"

"No."

"Yes, of course, we discussed it at your house. Well, it doesn't matter. You know how much I hate these business dinners, but it's important and I can't cancel it, believe me. You know I personally couldn't care less; what's in it for me? Believe me, I do it to ensure this country's cultural future, which certainly needs it . . . . Let me check . . . . Let's see, Tuesday. Wait, Tuesday is no good, but Wednesday you can choose, would you rather meet for lunch or for dinner. . . ? I assume you'll be here a few days."

"I can come only Monday. You'll have to tell me all these fascinating things some other time."

"Does this mean you don't want to see me? Are you angry? Your tone is a little . . . a little curt."

"You think so?"

"It seems there's been a misunderstanding between us, Angela. Frankly, you sound annoyed. I assure you Monday's dinner is crucial."

"I think I'm just beginning to know you, Miguel. I get the feeling I'll never be able to cheer for you again."

"Cheer for me? I don't understand."

"It's simple. I'm afraid you won't pull any more scarves out of your top hat."

"Angela, what are you talking about? I never pretended. . ."

"By the way, you looked great in the photo in *Breakthrough 36.*"

"Please, honey, don't be cruel. As you can imagine, I . . . Well, as luck would have it, that was Tonia, the director's wife. . . . It was a trick they played on us. You know how serious I am. Besides, I was representing the Foundation . . . . It's the fault of those reporters, always after the sensational. As I'm sure you'll understand, to me Tonia is nothing, what do you want me to say?"

"Yes, yes, I understand, of course! On the other hand, what's hard for me to understand is why you didn't tell me about your trip. Why did you disappear? What happened? Why didn't you call me back? What? "

"I was afraid of these questions, Angela. I was sure you'd ask me and, you see, I don't have an answer. I don't know, I just don't . . . . (Yes, Amparo, tell him I'll get to him in a minute.) Excuse me, Angela, I have to go. The Secretary is holding on the other line. If you come to Madrid, make sure you let me know, you know where I am. And if you need anything, don't hesitate to ask me. Because come what may we're friends, aren't we?"

CARME RIERA

The drizzling rain slowly lapped the windows while I hung up the phone, as if, almost noiselessly and imperceptibly, all the sadness in the world became one with mine. Beneath the afternoon's ashen light, the weather was changing: In the air the heart of autumn already beat at a slow rhythm. Feeling calmer, as if the rain liberated me, I began to write him a long letter. In rereading it I realized that the continuous reproaches— the penitent burlap in which I dressed my words—the spite that constantly emerged between lines, were counterproductive. They made my lovesickness all too obvious and, above all, exposed mercilessly, almost obscenely, the pain that, like a mutilation, his loss had caused me. Fortunately, I didn't send it. Nor did I have the strength to go to Madrid, Ingrid. His proper cold-ness, his verbal pyrotechnics, the gum he seemed to be chewing while we talked, led me to infer that he would invent another urgent meeting in order to avoid me. That frivolity of the expensive courtesan, trimmed with fluffy courtesy, scented with syrupy trivialities and gar-nished with cotton intended, no doubt, to swab my oozing sores—in case the puss might spatter him—hurt me more than the truth he tried to cover up: He didn't love me anymore. Nevertheless, I kept waiting for a miracle: a letter, a call, a visit, any sign of love that might provide me with an excuse to grant him a par-don for which he'd never ask and to renew our rela-tionship, because everything—music, books, flowers, even my own house—still reminded me of him.

A Matter of Self-Esteem

A mutual friend had run into him at some meeting at the ministry and conveyed his regards. She let me know that Miguel had asked about me and my well-being with great interest. I guessed that he might have insinuated our relationship to her. Her remark that "Miguel is very fond of you, you don't know how much" warned me against any temptation to confide in her, as my comments would have immediately been relayed to him. I only referred to his merits as a writer, but not to his human qualities. From my words she would actually infer that I didn't much care for his personality.

A few weeks later, early in December, Miguel called me. "May I dare request the pleasure of your voice?"

This pompous formality was spoken in the circumspect tone, unusual for him, of a wounded wolf. Perhaps, since he had plagiarized a line from Lorca,[19] intertextualizing and altering it, he was forced to compromise with humility for a moment. I tried to sound coldly polite. "You're welcome to try . . . the truth is that I wasn't expecting you."

"What's happened to you, Angela? Are you angry with me? Don't be unfair, my dear. If anything, it's me who should be offended. You came to Madrid and didn't even call me."

"You have so many obligations, and you didn't tell me when your secretary is allowed to put calls through . . . "

"Angela, for pity's sake, don't be unfair."

"I'm not being unfair at all. You're so busy that I'd have gotten in your way, and then I'd have felt guilty."

"I want to be honest with you, Angela. Sometimes I think I haven't treated you well. . . . That's why I've tried to correct the situation at the first opportunity . . . I'm the one that sometimes feels guilty without knowing exactly why . . . and this makes me uneasy."

"Take two Valium pills or, better yet, nitroglycerine. . .You can't get those without a prescription, though! But you must have a lot of doctor friends who could take care of that . . ."

"Angela, please!"

"I'm serious. I had to take them for quite a few days and, actually, they work pretty well . . ."

"I had forgotten how cruel you can be. No, Angela, you're not fair. You misjudge me. I love you very much, much more than you think. Everything about you is important to me."

"Really?"

"To be sure. Otherwise, why on earth would I make enemies on your account? Well, not exactly on your account, but because of you."

"I don't know what you're talking about."

"Why yes, enemies, and not exactly harmless either."

"Miguel, please, you don't have to protect my intellectual reputation or do me any favors. At this point, that's not necessary."

"You misunderstand me, my dear. Just yesterday, I defended you in front of Martínez Camorera. You know he's a very harsh critic. He was sitting next to me at the Machado awards banquet."[20]

"Oh, really? And what did Martínez Camorera say, may I ask? Because I don't think he's even read me. . ."

"From what he said it seems he has, dear."

"What did he say?"

"I'd rather not say, darling. We almost came to blows."

"How tough you are! Tell me, what did he say?"

"Something ridiculous, but you don't know how much it upset me. I was really hurt."

"How ridiculous was it?"

"I'd prefer not to say, my love. It's something silly that's going to hurt you and, above all, I don't want you to suffer."

"Phew! Don't worry. . . 'Pain, the ultimate form. . .' "

"What?"

"Nothing. Come on, what did he say?"

"Are you sure you want to know? Yes? He said: 'Angela Caminals is a washed-up writer.' You understand why I couldn't allow that."

"I understand, Miguel. Thank you very much."

And I hung up. The phone rang persistently thirty, forty times. Then, at intervals, three or four more, with a kind of purely testimonial rattle, not expecting an answer. Ingrid, I swear to you that I could never figure out the purpose of that call. Many people, among them our own colleagues at the conference, had complained bitterly about Miguel. Envy—he is a natural winner—made him a tempting target, and his vanity fueled his competitors' eagerness to hit the bull's-eye. I assure you that I have quietly diverted shots fired at him without passing him a bill. His was not only untimely, but it included an excessive luxury tax.

My Castilian translator is Camorera's childhood friend. I couldn't help mentioning the incident to her. Rocío was glad to help with any kind of verifications. A few hours later, I found out that the anecdote Miguel had told me was indeed true, but the actors' roles had been reversed. It was Camorera who defended me and Miguel who semi-seriously questioned the interest of my work and, with frivolous detachment, predicted my literary demise.

I don't think it's necessary to tell you those were dreadful days, filled with terrors. As if in a spell, ghosts performed macabre dances around me, monsters ridiculed me amidst guffaws and pirouettes, forcing me to reinterpret my relationship with Miguel, degrading it until it became a rotting morass in which only a sewer rat would feel at home. It was obvious that Miguel had never loved me and had made a fool of me from the beginning.

Ingrid, you can't imagine how much shame and how many regrets I felt as I recalled my complete surrender to him. I cruelly submitted every page of each of my books to the most morbid dissection. The manuscript I was working on, which I had promised to deliver before Christmas, lay unfinished on my study table. I felt absolutely incapable of writing a single line, because I suspected that in between its pages there was a trap lined with poisonous spikes ready to snap and cut off my fingers. And, at that point, my editor personally took me to see a psychiatrist friend of his.

More than a thousand hours spent in front of a wall, stirring the foulest obscenities inside me, brought me to the conclusion that I had been for Miguel, not only a disposable container, but a mirror in which he rehearsed his strategies of seduction. Thus, all the similarities he had pointed out with infinite complacency and ritual deliberation before I yielded to him became much clearer. Because it is, finally, in the mirror of the flesh that lovers recognize themselves, transgress the limits of the skin, and become one. However, in our case—in *his* case, as seducer and not as lover—my naked body must have reflected only his own image, while his didn't reflect mine. Once the secret was revealed, the magic disappeared and it was no longer possible to find a reflection that would encompass both of us. Narcissus quenches his thirst leaning over the lake, not plunging in it. The image he seeks is none other than his own, not that of his dead sister.[21] If he draws closer, if he gives in to the temptation of immersing himself in it, he'll make the mistake that will destroy him. His only alternative is to withdraw within himself, never to be alienated. The illusion that had kept our lives in constant tension throughout that month and a half disappeared suddenly, and with its disappearance came the death of my seductive power, although his remained intact. His behavior, even his last phone call, is easier to explain in this way. By pretending to have defended me before Camorera—he could never have imagined that I'd hear the other version—he tried to reestablish his battered reputation before me, for perhaps at some point he guessed that my mirror had shattered in a thousand pieces and that his seducer's image could never be put together again. I think he was only partly right; I'm pretty certain now that his refined, sophisticated plan to cause me pain by relaying Camorera's remark had more useful motives.

Ultimately, Ingrid, what a waste! So much energy spent on a useless passion! I don't know if you remember how Proust, in *Remembrance of Things Past*,[22] closes the chapter in which Swan finishes relating his love affair with Odette. It's a meditation that sums up perfectly the way I judge my romantic conduct: "To think that I have wasted the best years of my life, that I have longed to die and I have felt the greatest love of my existence, all for a woman who didn't suit me, who wasn't my type . . . ."

At this point, Ingrid, I'm very conscious that I've entered a new stage. My heart is almost as cold as my head. Common sense has gradually overcome neurotic melancholy and I'm quickly leaving behind the state of mind that tango lyrics describe and in which I, as a spoiled crybaby, so often indulged. I'm becoming a skeptic. You are the only person I approach without distrust; that's why I dare tell you that, despite everything, I quite often feel out of place, exposed. The values that a polished, bourgeois education tried to instill in me—loyalty, sincerity, the obsessive cult of truth— are no longer of any use to me; they're obsolete. Their marked devaluation in recent times has rendered them unprofitable. For many years I thought that my convictions would be a valid norm by which to judge the behavior of others as well as my own; that I should tailor my conduct to such convictions for reasons of basic ethics, making coexistence more bearable and allowing me to sleep, if not well, at least with a clear conscience, as Catholics say—and to feel a part of the value system that the civilized people of my social class uphold.

I don't know if these confessions will sound even more painful than the previous ones, considering that they show my utter helplessness more openly. I don't know the exact moment when I fell from the train and was thrown into a ditch; but I'm afraid I don't have the energy to get up again and climb onto the last car, or even to shake the dust and weeds off my clothes. Perhaps I have forever become a loner. I don't expect anything. Nothing in particular touches me. I see very few friends, I don't go to any social gatherings, I hardly leave the house. I do listen to music, almost all day long. More than ever, I've taken an interest in my collection of Galles,[23] which is growing, and in antiques. I just bought a positively beautiful sixteenth-century basin and now I have my eye on an incredible little Napoleonic chest. I take care of the garden. I savor the sunset whenever I can, seduced by those moments when the sky takes on that pale, milky hue, diffused with almost nocturnal blues and vague whites that remind me of your light. I often celebrate it with a champagne cocktail. Objects usually interest me more than people. For this reason, I try to surround myself with beautiful things, although my father's inheritance—on which I live—as you can imagine is shrinking too quickly. I don't care. In my own way, I try to seize from life even that which it doesn't want to relinquish. I could ask for little more. I avoid watching television altogether and read few newspapers, although sometimes I'm tempted by the culture section. This is how I learned that Miguel had sold out in a week the first edition of his latest novel *The Swan's Song*. Robert Saladrigas praised it in *La Vanguardia*,[24] describing it as a paraphrase of the nineteenth century, because its main character, a provincial woman writer, is a clear example of disenchanted romanticism, a degraded heroine in a degraded world.

Only two weeks ago I received a copy by mail, dedicated: "With the certainty that you will be my best critic." On the back cover, a blurb in large letters proclaimed the literary quality of the narration and particularly the originality of the subject, unexplored in Hispanic literature . . . Ingrid, you can imagine how eager I was to start the novel and how intensely I read it, underlining the paragraphs in which I sensed he referred to my appearance and moods, marking the pages in which Miguel reproduced fragments of our letters, transcribed our conversations or included passages stolen from the "charter documents of our love." And I realized that the character named Olga, the mature Catalan writer, as pretentious and corny as can be, was, if not my portrait, at least my caricature; and Sergio, the fashionable, triumphant novelist, brilliant and exceedingly intelligent, was he just as he sees himself, crowned with the halo of sainthood. You can imagine what happens from the moment the two meet to debate *La Regenta* at a round table discussion organized by the appropriate cultural entity and university of a northern city. Down to the last detail! The parallel between the two stories is sustained until the end of the first, that is, the night Olga surrenders to Sergio. The novel doesn't describe the intense, beautiful, exuberant night I remember, but rather an embarrassing and sterile fiasco. Olga, trapped in her prejudice, prudish and out of place, behaves ridiculously and stupidly and proves incapable of satisfying her passionate lover. When you read the book that I'll express-mail to you tomorrow morning— today, it's already Monday—you'll see how the author treats the poor crazy woman in the glorious finale.

But first, Ingrid, let me ask you a million questions, about an endless amount of doubts that have plagued me since the book fell into my hands. When did Miguel decide to write the novel—before or after we met in Valencia? Did I interest him only because he saw in me a ready-made character, a perfect fit for his plot? Or was it after we had met, when he noticed the similarities between us, that he couldn't resist the fascination of testing to what point literature is, always, subservient to life? Perhaps he intended to steer our relationship through preexisting channels toward an end consistent with the predetermined fate of his character . . . and that abrupt, unforeseen ending triggered our break-up. I don't know. I do know, however, that he used me to obtain first-hand information that provided him with a more human texture for his fictional creature. Maybe all these possibilities are nothing but complementary segments on the same kaleidoscope, which join and part depending on the focus and the motion. . .

Gridi, as much as it sometimes hurts, I continue to read *The Swan's Song*. To find, hidden between the lines, whatever plausible explanation; to know more about myself; to gain back a lost year; to reunite with that dead self of which I only am, in a way, a surviving part—the other part disintegrated, torn to shreds, during those horrible months—I still purposely search for myself in the pages of the novel. I'm very interested, Ingrid, in your opinion as to whether the protagonist of this book is really me or I've mistakenly recognized myself in its mirror-like pages. Perhaps it's my anxiety to prevail, despite everything, in Miguel's memory, the need to justify still his sudden change of attitude, that forces me to reread his story again and again.

I don't deny, Ingrid, that throughout these days I've been tempted to emulate Serpieri—do you remember Visconti's *Senso?*[25]—but this would only enhance his posthumous fame. The possibility of a lawsuit has also occurred to me. I could base it on the violation in his novel of my right to privacy or on his publicizing our relationship in the sensationalist press, but either action would just increase Miguel's popularity and the sales of his book, to the detriment of my reputation.

Now I realize that I never told you his last name, although I'm sure you guessed it long ago. Miguel isn't too common a name among contemporary writers and since, of course, it isn't Delibes, it could only be Orbaneja. An extensive interview with him appeared in the Sunday supplement of today's—yesterday's—*La Nación*.[26] In it he announces that in a month he'll travel to Denmark to give a series of lectures at the Universities of Copenhagen, Odense, and Aarhus; at the same time, he'll write reports that will be disseminated to the major newspapers in Spain and Latin America through the agency EFE, prior to the publication of a travel book on Scandinavia "whose far smoother light," I'm quoting verbatim, "which brings objects closer to us and shortens distances, I desperately long for . . ."

I'm sure Miguel will do everything he can to meet and befriend you. Don't be surprised. I spoke to him about you a great deal, about your fondness for Spanish literature, your excellent relations with Scandinavian intellectuals—especially your friendship with Lunkvist, keyholder to the door of the Nobel Prize to which, of course, he aspires in the near future—not to mention your intelligence and stunning appeal. I assure you that he'll try to find in you another mirror in which he can admire himself as he pleases, and that he'll take pleasure in showing you an endless number of similarities. But he won't deceive you, because the pedantry and arrogance that, strangely enough, worked well on me, perhaps because I sensed behind that mask an almost sickly and pathological weakness, won't captivate you. It was his supposedly vulnerable side that truly seduced me. Maybe he always used it as a trump card with women. It's possible that Miguel, striving for a more intimate atmosphere, will talk about me at length, in the most delicate terms. Don't forget that, although vain, he is diabolically clever. Forgive me, Ingrid, I was going to put you on guard once again. I know that isn't the least bit necessary. When it comes to men, you have much more experience than I do, and you play with marked cards. The game is definitively yours.

A few hours ago, in the mid-afternoon—now it's after two o'clock in the morning—I said I'd ask you a favor. I think the time has come to tell you what it is about, although I'm sure you've nearly guessed it. No, I'm not asking you to give Miguel a taste of his own medicine, that phony medicine he used on me. To seduce him would be child's play for you and to dump him the easiest thing in the world. Moreover, I'm sure it would barely scratch him. At times I think I must have been one of the few fools he's ever taken to bed, which makes me, in a way, even angrier. Only a patsy like me would fail to see through him, with his portable altar under his arm, ready to perform a meticulous immolation ceremony with the first gullible sap to come his way, offering herself as a victim of his elephantine narcissism. It seems to me that in your case we may rule out this possibility, although if you find yourself in this situation and the mood strikes you, do whatever you feel is most convenient. Not in vain have you amused yourself with heroines of Spanish drama who must avenge their lost honor . . . . and, look, now you have the chance to play the role yourself on my behalf. I don't advise you, for the joyful event, the second movement of Mozart's Piano Concerto no. 21— oh, yes, our favorite for telephone intimacy—because he'll confuse it, as he already did, with "something by Brahms." Rather play something more ad hoc, like "Pomp and Circumstance," for example. . . .

Anyway, to the point. What I want to ask you is much more subtle. As you'll see, Miguel has the prodigious ability to change into himself everything he touches, to appropriate other people's ideas with charming spontaneity, to express opinions of others as if they were his own and, whenever it suits him, to intertextualize anything he wants. He never disagrees. So, it wouldn't surprise me if he wholly concurred with your point of view, marveling at your common taste and identifying with your words. Nor do I find it difficult to imagine his first chronicle: chock-full of keen observations about your idiosyncracies, of historical and literary references that are brilliant but, above all, *original*, and that you will have suggested to him. Imagine how great it would be if you convinced him of Isak Dinesen's nostalgia for the cliffs of the Fionia plain, if you talked to him about the pornographic expressionism of Dreyer's early films, or the explosive, icy eroticism of Thorwaldsen's torsos, for which his fans call him the Danish Rodin. . . . Perhaps it would also be worthwhile to slip in some bedroom gossip; he loves it and knows how to take advantage of it admirably. Why not refer to Andersen's *fou*[27] love for Oerstaad, aroused when the latter expounded on magnetic machines? Or the necklace of *quanta* that Neils Bohr gave to Mata Hari as a souvenir of their shared binges. . . . Of course, I should expect a much more subtle erudition and greater refinement from you, as you show him certain aspects of your country through a distorted lens.[28]

One month is left, Ingrid, only a month; but already I look forward to reading Miguel's reports, plagued with errors if not with sheer nonsense that no doubt will infuriate Lunkvist, thus diminishing the chances that one day Miguel will find himself in tails before the King of Sweden to receive the Nobel Prize.

A Matter of Self-Esteem

In truth, it isn't his making himself ridiculous—with your help, of course—that will satisfy me the most, but rather the certainty that, in his infinite haughtiness, he'll draw a misogynistic moral: You can't trust the judgment of women, because it's a quality they don't possess.

Right now, as soon as I finish this letter, I'll check the contents of my wine cellar. I want to be sure to have a Pomery when the moment arrives. I'll drink to your health, my dear, I promise you.

I don't have to tell you that, as always, I'm at your service, now more than ever, and that you can ask anything of me. You know I love you very much and I send you lots of kisses.

ANGELA

NOTES

1. Vallvidrera is a wealthy suburb of Barcelona. "A Matter of Self-Esteem" is set in Barcelona and Valencia, another important Spanish city on the Mediterranean.

2. Joan Maragall was a major turn-of-the-century Catalan poet. *The Intruder* is a drama by Maurice Maeterlinck, a famous Belgian playwright of the same period.

3. Miguel de Unamuno was one of the most influential Spanish philosophers and a contemporary of Maragall.

4. *La Regenta* (The Regent's Wife), written by Leopoldo Alas and published in 1885, was a realist novel ahead of its time in its recognition of sexual desire as a major part of the psychological motivations of its characters. An English translation exists under the same Spanish title. Ana Ozores is the heroine of *La Regenta*.

5. *Clarín* was the pen name of Leopoldo Alas, author of *La Regenta*.

6. Benito Pérez Galdós was one of the major realist novelists of nineteenth century Spain.

7. Angela and Miguel refer to Cervantes' *Don Quixote*; Alonso Quijano is the protagonist's name before he becomes a knight errant.

Notes

8. *Doña Perfecta* (1876) and *Misericordia* (1897) are two novels by Pérez Galdós (see Note 6) that have older female protagonists. The titles are, in fact, the two women's first names.

9. Poem by Ausias March, the first important poet to write in Catalan. Catalan is the language spoken, with several variations, in Catalonia, Valencia, and the Balearic Islands. He lived in the fifteenth century.

10. This paragraph plays with lines from the poem *Canción del pirata* (Pirate's Song), by the nineteenth-century Spanish poet José de Espronceda.

11. Pere Serafí was a sixteenth-century Catalan poet; Jordi de Sant Jordi was a fifteenth-century Valencian poet who wrote music and love songs at the height of the so-called Catalan Renaissance.

12. Pedro Salinas was a twentieth-century poet and essayist.

13. Karoline Frederike Luise Maximiliane von Günderrode was a late nineteenth-century author of poetry, prose, and letters.

14. Calixto and Melibea are the young lovers in *La Celestina. Tragicomedia de Calixto y Melibea*, a novel in dialogue by Fernando de Rojas published in 1499.

15.   Antoni Gaudí was a famous turn-of-the-century architect known for his modernistic buildings in Barcelona, especially the temple of *La Sagrada Familia* (The Holy Family).

16. The line "The past forever swept away to begin anew with you" is from a song by the French singer Edith Piaf.

17.   Riera refers to the myth of Faust, best known in the versions of Christopher Marlowe in the sixteenth century and Johann Wolfgang von Goethe in the romantic period.

18.   The sentence means "Enlightenment always comes from the North."

19. Frederico García Lorca was a celebrated poet and playwright who was killed in 1936, at the onset of the Spanish Civil War.

20. The Antonio Machado Prize for Short Stories is named after this twentieth-century Spanish poet and awarded annually.

21.   Narcissus' "dead sister" is the nymph Echo who, because of her unreciprocated love for him, pined away until only her voice remained.

22.   *Remembrance of Things Past* was the masterwork of well-known turn-of-the-century French novelist Marcel Proust.

23.   "Galles" is an incorrect spelling of Gallé. Emile Gallé was a French artist famous for his work with glass and ceramics. His style is representative of the modernistic school that blossomed in the early twentieth century.

24.   *La Vanguardia* is one of the main Spanish newspapers.

25.   Luchino Visconti was one of the most widely recognized Italian film directors.   His movie *Senso* (1954) tells the story of Countess Livia Serperi, who is seduced by an Austrian army leiutenant in 1866, while Italy is under occupation.   When revolution breaks out, she's torn between her patriotism and her feelings for an enemy of her country. In the end, realizing that the Austrian officer doesn't love her and has simply used her in order to flee the army, she reports him as a deserter and he is executed.   Angela is similarly tempt-ed to denounce Miguel, presumably for defamation or plagiarism.

26.   *La Nación* (The Nation) is a Spanish periodical.

27.   *Fou* means "mad" in French. The use of foreign words is one of Miguel's affectations, which Angela parodies here.

28.   Hans Christian Andersen, the famous nine-teenth-century author of children's stories, never had a homosexual affair with Hans Christian Oersted, a physicist born almost a century earlier; nor was nuclear

Notes

physicist Niels Bohr involved with the legendary spy
Mata Hari—the reference to the "necklace of *quanta*" is
sheer nonsense: *quanta* are units of energy. Novelist
Isak Dinesen (a pen name for Karen Dinesen Blixen-
Finecke) isn't known for her longing for the Fionia
plain, but for her writings about Africa. John Louis
Emil Dreyer was an astronomer born in the eighteenth
century rather than a modern film director, and his
contemporary Albert Bertel Thorwaldsen, although a
sculptor, specialized in religious and historical
subjects and bore no similarity with the French sculptor
Rodin. Angela is instructing Ingrid to give Miguel false
information about Danish intellectuals, so that he will
later reproduce that information in his books and thus
discredit himself.

Mon Semblable, Mon Frère

For Gonzalo Torrente Ballester,
who asked me to dance.

I HAVE JUST READ in the *Grand Daily Newspaper* a story by Juan José Millás titled "The Little Corpse of R. J."[1] I don't want to postpone a day longer my report on the facts of this case. Two years ago, when that meddling young teacher published her dissertation, which was full of vapid falsehoods about Rafel's life, I came close to revealing everything I know. If I didn't, it was because at the time, on the verge of my retrospective exhibit in Madrid, I didn't want to become involved in a scandal. I believe I did the right thing. Perhaps if I had spilled the beans I wouldn't have won the National Award in Plastic Arts. Lluis Recasens, first cousin of

Rafel and a great fan of his work, was a member of the jury.

The prize came to me late in my career, no doubt, but it helped to arouse the curiosity of my countrymen about my painting, which up to that point had been much more appreciated abroad, and increased its market value nationwide. I was able to take a few months off to indulge my vanity. When it comes to my painting, which is what I really care about, I'm neither Rafel's master nor a surviving disciple. Despite my age, I continue to work with enthusiasm.

The truth is that Millás has been misinformed. Nonetheless, there is no question that Rafel and I could easily recognize ourselves in his story, although I never said goodbye to Rafel. I didn't go to see the casket, covered with the Catalan flag, on public display at the Sant Jaume Palace. I learned of his suicide late because, even though Calatayud, where I was at the time, gets the national papers, I didn't read any that day, not even the *Grand Daily Newspaper*, which printed the news on the front page. But I know the exact time of his death, even the moment when his agony started. It happened in the early morning, around 3:00 A.M. At 5:35 A.M. everything was over. At that same hour I checked into the emergency room of the Calatayud County Hospital with a perforated stomach that initially seemed fatal. I really believed I was done for. At last they managed to revive me with a series of transfusions. Fortunately, I have one of the most common blood types and the hospital found a host of donors among the local unemployed. If I'm still alive it is thanks to a lack of welfare benefits that is surprising in such a rich county.

I spent almost a week recovering in Calatayud and heard about Rafel's death upon my return to Barcelona, after enjoying a moderate commercial success at the exhibition room of the Rural Bank of Aragón y La Rioja. It was much more than a terrible shock or a devastating blow, as we say in these situations. It was as though I had been split in two.

As for Millás's account, I must say that he isn't the first to make a profit from our lives. The first was Bonomini in *Secret Stories*, except that book was sold only in Argentina, almost five years ago, shortly after Rafel's death. At the time, despite the "kind regards" the publisher sent along, I didn't suspect that the story titled "Self-Portraits" might be the first effort to set the record straight—on my behalf, of course. On the contrary, I thought it a simple coincidence.

There are inside me, just as inside most people, particularly artists, infinite possibilities. Actually, we're just one or two of the many individuals we might have been, and so there was nothing unusual in the fact that Rafel's story and mine coexisted in Angel Bonomini's mind. Moreover, since I went to Latin America I've been getting a lot of books from there. Some of the publishers I contacted, because they were friends of friends, were nice enough, or as Rafel would say, unscrupulous enough, to include my name in their lists of recommended authors; consequently, I'm swamped now and then with their promotional materials, which I sell as quickly as possible. Besides the certainty that, at my age, new books will bring no surprises, there's the problem of lack of space, for I not only work but also live in my shop. I still don't know the reason why Bonomini's book attracted me. Perhaps it was the engraving, a small vignette of five horses reproduced at the bottom of the cover. Two of them are perfect Siamese brothers, each with two heads. Their manes have been transformed into roots, or perhaps they are roots that have become manes. Metamorphoses have always fascinated me, to the point that a couple of years ago I myself did some drawings on this subject. This explains why I didn't get rid of the book. However, I didn't read it right away. It wasn't till four or five months later that I started.

I know for a fact that Millás has connections in Argentina. Perhaps he too received the book with "kind regards," for there is no question that his account is inspired by Bonomini's. Who knows if he wrote it with the intention of breaking my silence and forcing me to become involved at last. As for Angel Bonomini, a remarkable writer (read *Secret Stories* and see for yourself), I've had no contact with him; all I know is that he could have heard of my relationship with Rafel through a third person.

The telephone has been ringing nonstop since it woke me up this morning. Maybe it's Valbuena. If he has read "The Little Corpse" he'll want to see me right away, fearing that it may be me who started this whole thing. Or perhaps it's Enric, in a state of hysteria: "You swore by Rafel's memory you'd keep quiet." I dread the crying scene. When a widower is a widow he's even more faithful. I have no intention of picking up the phone. Screw them. At least, not before I finish this report.

A certain poetic gift guides the tip of my pen when I write prose—when I "pontificate," Rafel would have objected, always ready to "circumcise" anyone who stood in his way. It was actually he who often advised me to write in prose. I never paid any attention to him, not even when he stubbornly persisted in the idea of co-writing a bilingual novel with me. . . .

I believe the moment has come—my dear Enric, sometimes one must go back on his promises—for me to say the last word to those who have already started on the warpath, before critics and professors flock like vultures to feast on the rotting corpses.

Rafel and I became friends in the mid-fifties. Neither of us could remember who had introduced us or where we had met, although it probably happened at the University, during the discussions that took place after classes. What I distinctly remember is that we weren't in the same class and that for a long time we only knew each other by sight and didn't even exchange greetings in the street. I deeply detested his arrogant demeanor, his cocky, patronizing air of handsome big brother. Later I found out that he felt the same way about me. It was at the seminar open to fourth-year students and taught by Canals in 1956, the year he came in, that we initiated an academic relationship that would soon also become personal. Rafel and I had grown inseparable at the end of '56–'57. I still remember vividly our walks in the old district, our visits to an endless number of joints where we even made some friends. I remember coming back on those drunken early mornings, I to my place, he to the dorm, both happy and staggering, our heads simmering with alcohol and plans. That was the year—the last I would spend in Barcelona and the year of Rafel's graduation—when Canals would recommend him as a teaching assistant, hoping that he might get a grant to conduct research. Everything boded a brilliant academic future for Rafel; under Canals's wing, he would be able to compete successfully for a permanent position after he finished his doctorate. Luck seemed to smile upon me too, although my parents didn't take my artistic pretensions seriously. My family, unlike Rafel's, belonged to the winning side and was wealthy,[2] which gave me a few bellyaches but otherwise made things very smooth for me. By May, I extracted from them (without having to beg too much) a promise that I could complete my last year of University by studying abroad, first at La Sorbonne and then at Oxford.

Rafel and I spent the summer of 1957 together at a country house my parents owned in the area of

Mon Semblable, Mon Frère

Tarragona. If I record this fact it's because eventually it would be very important for both of us. No doubt, our daily contact was decisive in my developing a serious interest in literature, without giving up my desire to paint. Rafel's enthusiasm must have infected me. Above all, he wanted to be a writer. Although at the time he had not yet told me, he began to write when he was a child living in Narbonne. His parents had moved there at the outbreak of the war, but in the mid-forties they came back, so that their children might be educated in the language of their forefathers. This admirable faithfulness of Senyor Recasens i Collbató to his mother tongue would be, by one of those ironies of life, crucial to my later relationship with Rafel and, of course, to our literary careers.

His poems, which became available to me in July (that summer Rafel had been staying at my home for a month), were formally perfect and unusually brilliant, but they weren't written in Catalan; they were written in French, in the excellent French of a real connoisseur who is familiar with the most genuine idioms. In addition, they were perfectly scanned and reminiscent of Baudelaire's *Parisian Tableaux*.[3] My telling him so was the best compliment I could ever pay him, for his intention was no other than to follow the master to the point of being indistinguishable from him. The truth is that at the time Rafel was already fairly eccentric. His literary tastes, unlike those of most intellectuals, which didn't go beyond Carles Riba, Carner, Antonio

Machado, or Lorca,[4] usually coincided with mine; we
shared our childhood fondness for reading, sparked in
both of us by a tuberculosis that broke out conveniently
at the peak of our literary frenzy, that is, at the beginning of our adolescence.

Just to flatter him, I started to translate his poems
into Catalan. I remember that on his birthday, August
25, I gave him a notebook bound in a hard grey cover
with my rendition of his texts and my own illustra-
tions. And I also remember that at that stage in my life,
having been around quite a bit, I was surprised by the
pressure of his strong, sinewy hand on my back, right
on the tendon. Rafel really liked my translations. He
tried to imitate them and gave up. He congratulated
me for two reasons: not only did my version appear to
be flawless—I had achieved perfect pitch, the appropriate tempo and the right expression—but it also revealed
a great poetic ability. As far as he was concerned, he
should definitely write in Catalan. For the first time, as
he read my translations, he didn't regret that his family had insisted on going back to their country, depriv-
ing him of *les délices de la France*.[5]

In mid-September Rafel presented me with a series
of poems in Catalan, dedicated to me. They seemed like
school exercises. They lacked any kind of poetic life.
They were wooden. I wish I had never confessed my
disappointment to him. That same afternoon, Rafel left
Altafulla without even saying goodbye to my mother.

In October, before my trip to Paris, I received a

brief letter. He apologized for having left without a word and referred to his linguistic dependence, added an obscenity about his "Gallic neurosis" and encouraged me to write. I didn't answer. Before I left, I stopped by his house to say goodbye, but he no longer lived there. At the University Canals told me that he had gone to Lérida to see his family because his mother was seriously ill.

Around Christmas I got an endless letter from him by way of my father. It was a kind of inventory. A confession. A contrite prayer. A resolution to make amends in the coming year, and so on. At the end of May, just before flying back to Barcelona, I received in Oxford a copy of Rafel's French poems in my Catalan translation. Nowhere did the author indicate that the Catalan version was mine or that the original had been written in French. In an obscure note he referred to me as "his dear José Joaquín"[6] and assured me that Canals had vouched most emphatically for his work. I answered him without showing displeasure or irritation. Instead of Rafel, I called him *Fernán*. I also alluded, in passing, to the many quills of *The Seagull*. Years later, when our friends were too drunk to interfere with our speeches, he and I would still argue over the seagull's quills and the Böhl de Faber family.[7]

My literary debut was as a translator from a language that, while not at all unknown to me, I have never felt to be my own. In spite of that, I find it much more suitable for poetry than Castilian itself. The latter—my native language—is too harsh. The absence of neutral vowels considerably undercuts its musical possibilities. Besides, many of its words are so long that they weigh it down. Rafel and I used to talk about this often, especially when I went back to Oxford and our magazine *The Dancing Egg*, which had seen its second issue—an unprecedented event in poetry, particularly in that context of linguistic persecution and lyric mediocrity—established Rafel as a young master. It was then that, encouraged by my own success—the French original may have been his, but the Catalan version was mine—I began to write. Spurred by Rafel, I worked on a book of poems in Castilian. He himself urged me to be faithful to my mother tongue. Later I suspected that there was a selfish purpose to his advice: his fear that I might overshadow him if I wrote in Catalan. He even appealed to my family ties with Campoamor[8] and to my roots in central Spain; and, as a definitive argument, he mentioned that the possibility of worldwide readership certainly justified favoring the language of the majority. I wish he had been in my place! His words struck me as cynically refined. But that's how Rafel was, and I chose not to embark on a debate that might have been endless.

And so I published my first book of poems, *Outskirts*, in 1961. It went largely unnoticed. Only one local magazine controlled from a distance by the distinguished Canals reviewed it. It did it justice. A year later, before the publisher—Cortada was his name—

remaindered it, he sent me a letter informing me that out of an edition of 750 copies, 50 had been sold. The other 700, 688 to be precise, were burned in a funeral pyre that Rafel, Valbuena, and I lit in front of the Greek dock of Ampurias one night under a full moon.

I decided to devote myself exclusively to painting. I had wasted too much time painstakingly composing the two series that made the book and that I considered quite good. At least I had taken advantage of the lesson learned in England from the poets of the thirties, whose influence hadn't yet reached this country, which was still impermeable to innovative European trends and interested only in the Spanish sonnet and modernism. One of the few exceptions was Rafel, who, being a devoted fan of Baudelaire, had come to Eliot through their mutual admiration for their Parisian *semblable*.[9]

The truth is that, at this point, I don't know if my own discovery of Eliot preceded or followed Rafel's, or which one of us squeezed *The Wasteland* for all that it's worth. All I know is that the poems in *Water Over the Dam*, published in 1962, were composed directly in Catalan with borrowed lines—rejects from *Outskirts*, a book to which he had contributed and about which he had elaborate opinions. This incident drove me away from Rafel, although some strange scruple prevented me from making any claims and suing him for plagiarism. I simply stopped seeing him. It wasn't difficult. Valbuena, closer to Rafel than to me, tried to reconcile us. He, who knew that I had translated *The Dancing Egg*, assumed that professional jealousy had triggered the dispute. I told him the truth. He didn't believe me. On the contrary, he thought that it was *Water Over the Dam* that had influenced *Outskirts* rather than the other way around.

According to critics and even to textbook authors, for by now Rafel's work appears in school curricula next to that of Ausiàs March and Espriu,[10] *Water Over the Dam* marks the beginning of his second stage, followed by ten years of puzzling silence that no scholar has been able to explain and to which I, however, may have the key. Researchers [sic] simply state that for a while Rafel devoted himself to painting and at the same time taught at the University. In their view, this is the reason why there is no literary output throughout this period.

I can see him walk into my study defeated and with his head lowered, on a winter afternoon in 1964, under the pretext of informing me of some political event. A couple of days later I painted him like that, with that dejected air and sullen scowl, in front of a mirror that also reflected my own face as I painted him. No doubt, Bonomini must have reproduced this scene in "Self-Portraits." And I tried to capture in our faces and our features the resemblance that time had accentuated even more. I believe that my portrait impressed him, not so much for the quality that I think it achieved, as for its ambiance, for the blend of affection and contempt, rejection and love, hostility and trust implied in the way we look at each other. "As if we were one person," he said suddenly, and left. Two days later he came back and asked me for a space to set up his easel. Rafel either smeared the canvas or copied my strokes. There wasn't a shred of originality in him. Soon he gave it up. Sometime later he would stop by for a drink in the afternoon or go out for dinner with friends from his circle, poets, critics, and professors with whom he showed me and himself off, like a sparkling false diamond. This is the period of his sudden poetic raptures in the shape of *espineles*[11] to which I, prompted by the audience, felt obligated to respond on the spot. It is also the period of our best poems, generated by warm conversation and drinks. As I'm not sure if they were his or mine, I believe I can honestly consider them ours. What I know is that the spontaneous poetic rush of those moments led me to write once again and to make the mistake of telling Rafel, who in turn confessed that he too had resumed his writing.

Throughout those months we spent nervous, feverish hours devoted to our activities. Both of us were obsessed with a lengthy poem that, by means of a dramatic monologue—Eliot and the English poets of the thirties once again—purported to give an account of life, of our lives and those of other people of our age and condition. During this last stage my dealings with Rafel were more frequent and also more productive. His unquestionable poetic talent, his intelligence, his ability to seduce, could make him an extraordinary conversationalist if he was in a good mood and a tyrannical soliloquist if he was inspired.

In those days Rafel seemed bent on cultivating exclusively his positive image. Thus, our conversations were always not only brilliant but also enriching, and often we had a cluster of young men ready to be dazzled by our know-how. Among them was Enric, at the time a student of Rafel's and still too inexperienced to suit the master's taste.

We promised ourselves that we would show each other *the product, the monster, the great dinosaur*, only after having crossed absolutely all our t's. I finished sooner than Rafel—two months sooner, if I'm not mistaken. He insisted that he couldn't wait to peruse my text and for that reason he was rushing to end his poem somewhat abruptly. The truth is, that on the night when we finally decided to share our work, I was quite shocked. Rafel came to the study completely plastered, his speech slurred, with a folder under his arm and accompanied by Enric. Incapable of reading, he gave me the papers to read aloud. Enric didn't know the original either and, given his rising star as a favorite pupil, was even more eager than myself to see it as soon as possible. I started to read right away. The poems were splendid. They assimilated perfectly the lesson of our masters. In addition, they had a rhythm that matched impeccably the narrative tone; they resembled mine a great deal—and, this time, there was no question of plagiarism—but they were written in French.

Rafel, despite being egregiously drunk, listened to me intently. In his eyes there was a plea that only I could understand: "This is the last time, I promise," it seemed to say.

"Translate my work, for goodness' sake," he burst out suddenly. I absolutely refused.

"Look for a publisher in Paris. You have some contacts there," I suggested.

"I've already tried that, don't think I haven't," he replied, slightly twisting his mouth with a mocking expression that I knew well. "Nobody will pay a franc for it. They aren't interested. My poems are *dejà vu.*"

And he showed me the letters from two editors, dated a few months back. I surmised, therefore, that he had finished the poem, not at the same time as I did, but earlier, and that he had lied. But, why?

"I want to hear yours, now. Let Enric read it, you'd ruin it for sure. The only thing you read well is my stuff," he mumbled, helping himself to another glass of bourbon.

Enric put on a pair of silly glasses that made him look like the favorite son-in-law of a bossy widow—he still does, after many years—and began to read. His throaty voice and his terrible accent from Vallgossona did nothing at all for my poems, which called for a conversational rhythm and a spontaneous, completely colloquial tone.

"Enough, enough!" Rafel cried from his chair,

choking on his words. "You botch everything you touch, my boy. You're cuter when you shut up, Quinquín . . ." [12]

Enric stopped suddenly. I found the joke to be in very poor taste. Although Rafel had picked on his young devotee in public before, he had never humiliated him like this in my presence.

"Leave us alone, Enric, please," he added with a more conciliatory manner.

Enric left awkwardly, without saying goodbye—on this point he took after his master. I had never seen Rafel look so defeated.

"I'm sorry," he said, "I've put you through this grotesque scene. Sometimes he drives me crazy. I despise him, but he's the only one who puts up with me, the only one of them all who cares about me. Believe it or not, I find this even more aggravating. If I'm still with him it's only because I can fuck him whenever I please. . . . Our marital fights, his submissiveness, even his passivity in bed, make me sick . . . "

That was the first time Rafel had openly referred to his sexual relationship with Enric, although in truth all of us suspected it.

"Forgive me," he insisted. "Let me take a shower and, if it isn't too much trouble, fix me a big cup of coffee. I want to listen to your poems with the greatest attention."

The slimy bird with iron claws, that hideous dawn both Rafel's and my poems alluded to, was already scratching the window panes when, at last, Rafel was ready to listen. I tried to read slowly and intently, but my poem attained its full potential only when he recited it, extracting every possible meaning and truly recreating it.

"It's splendid," he reassured me. "Much better than *Outskirts*. You must publish it right away. I'll bet you anything that you'll revolutionize Castilian poetry."

I drank too much, to celebrate my success, while Rafel dozed on my sofa. I don't remember at all what happened between 6:00 A.M. and noon. All I know is that I woke up naked in my bed with a completely dry mouth. The room was in a state that suggested a turbulent, shared night. The dirty sheets lay on the ground. Rafel was gone. Up on an empty easel, in place of a canvas, he had left his poems in an open folder with the following note: "I depend on you, *mon semblable, mon frère*."

My book, for all of Rafel's encouraging predictions, failed to interest any prestigious publisher.

"Perhaps with a preface or, at least, a letter of recommendation by Aleixandre[13] somebody would take a chance on it," a critic friend of mine suggested.

With admirable expediency and without my asking, Rafel managed to secure it.

Aleixandre, most generously—later I found out that he was generous with everyone—wrote a few pages of introduction steeped in praise and a letter that recommended the publication of *Symphony in Grey Minor*.

The truth is that Rafel behaved like a real friend and didn't bring up at all the issue of the translation.

The Boscán Prize would be announced in Barcelona in June. It was a matter of total indifference to me. I did know that Rafel, Venancio, and other acquaintances were members of the jury, but I hadn't submitted my manuscript. I was astonished when Del Arco, from *La Vanguardia*, called me in the wee hours of the night to interview me as the winner.

Rafel, without telling anyone, had made copies of the manuscript and submitted it. Now I wouldn't have any problem getting it published. That same morning, euphoric after celebrating my success with him and convinced of our brotherhood, I began to translate his poems.

It took me almost a month. One evening I invited him to dinner and then I read them aloud. He was extremely pleased with the translation. Not only had I been as conscientious as possible, but I had taken the liberty of improving a few of the original verses.

"It sounds terrific in this language that eludes me, this damned language of shopkeepers and manufacturers," Rafel said when I finished, and then added sarcastically, "but the credit, my friend, is all yours."

Rafel's book—perhaps I should say our book—came out long before mine, barely a month after I had completed the translation. Its success, both commercial and critical, was unanimous. Critics went as far as to deem his period of silence worthwhile and to anoint him definitively. Rafel, even though he didn't mention my contribution, dedicated the book to me: "To my dear friend, José Ignacio Díaz de Benjumea, *mon semblable, mon frère*." For the first time, Castilian literary magazines—all the *Isles, Cantos, Spanish Poems, Son Armadans Papers*, and others I have forgotten—praised this young author who wrote in a language still humiliated, abused, and mistreated. Moreover, some reviews placed him above Salvador Espriu.

My own collection, *Symphony in Grey Minor*, wasn't published till the late fall. The Boscán Prize followed a complicated procedure whereby the winning poems came out almost a year after receiving the award. My book, despite the eulogy written by Aleixandre—to whom Rafel had introduced me one evening in Velintonia—once again went completely unnoticed, regardless of the fact that at Rafel's suggestion I sent copies with his card attached to every publisher that in his estimation might send me a commentary. Only one of them responded; somebody named Roberto Lamuela compared my text to Recasens': Rafel had taken it upon himself to send a letter—or so he told me; perhaps he had only written it—pointing out to Lamuela— "the mule" or "*Monsieur le Brayer*," as he used to call him in our conversations—that the coincidences in our work stemmed from our common masters; from a similar understanding of the poetic phenomenon; and, above all, from the use of colloquial idioms that, even if they came from different languages, cropped up in our ordinary conversations.

It was this notion that led Rafel to suggest a bilingual novel: He would write it in French and I would translate it later, besides adding my own section in Castilian. I refused. I told him I'd rather write it myself in his fraudulent language. In my case, writing was a minor vocation that didn't greatly interest me. My main passion was painting, which allowed me to reflect my own world much more effectively, without language barriers.

Rereading this report—for that's all it claims to be—I realize I haven't mentioned that throughout this period I had exhibits in various cities of the country and that my painting—unlike my literary work—did achieve recognition. Around those years, 1973 or 1974, I changed dealers. The new one, a smart German named Hans Hinterhausen, wanted to break into the American market and arranged a tour around several cities in the United States. It was there that for the first time I exhibited one of my best pieces, the portrait of Rafel and myself together. It was purchased by an Argentinean collector, the extremely powerful Gianfranco Branchiosi. Branchiosi and I became friends and he invited me for a lengthy stay in his house in Mar del Plata. Often Gianfranco urged me to tell him about Barcelona, so I revealed to him my tortuous linguistic relationship with Rafel. Now it dawns on me that maybe he shared my confidences with his friends and that's how they reached Bonomini. It really doesn't matter. I hope that this account will put an end to the issue once and for all.

Mon Semblable, Mon Frère

I remained in South America for almost three years. News from Rafel came only from time to time. His courses bored him. He spent his energy in night orgies, getting drunk till he collapsed. In one of his letters he announced that he had resumed writing: "And this time I write about us, as a catharsis," he stated, "out of pure necessity, in order to know who I am and to not go insane." With my answer I sent him a poem, the last one I've written; for with that poem I closed every gap, precluded any possibility of continuity, and, of course, terminated our cooperation. After I finished it I knew it was good, probably the best of all I had written or could write in the future, provided I hadn't already signed my poetic death sentence. I wrote it in Spanish and immediately translated it into Catalan. This shopkeepers' language, as Rafel would say, has a strange texture that makes everything sound as if it were named for the first time. Could it be these devilish neutral vowels that Castilian lacks? Let's assume this isn't true and that when I translate I'm simply able to create an ambiguous, suggestive text with a sense of the language.

At this point I know that my literary gift served Rafel exclusively, who otherwise — and perhaps this brought about his self-destruction — would have been but an ignored Sunday evening versifier, writing in French, to boot.

As I stated before, I wrote my best poem and sent it to Rafel as a gift, so that he could publish it wherever he wished; if he didn't, however, he would never have a chance to sign another poem, for that would be his last one, his farewell to the literary world, his definitive goodbye: in other words, his legacy, in which the individual poet leaves his self behind and examines his made-up identity and the humiliations he has inflicted upon his twin brother, who has his same height and brownish eyes and, perhaps, unbeknownst to him, the same tendency to a nefarious vice. Reflected in the mirror—just as in the painting—and juxtaposed against Rafel's face, there was my own; and there were also my pettiness, my humiliating compromises with mediocrity, my shameful concessions to routine, the sour taste of myself oozing from our united images. Who knows if that lovers' quarrel between Rafel and Enric that I had witnessed in my study inspired my poem and also the dramatic monologue that ends by suggesting that, sometimes, it is necessary to kill in order to survive. To murder the more literary self. To give up writing—to give up literature—forever, as the only therapy to avoid real suicide.

Rafel received the criticism award *The Golden Letter*. Every prize given that year in Catalonia went to his extremely brief collection of 235 poems, in which only the title, *The Mirrors*, was his own. He didn't even bother to send me a copy.

When I came back to Barcelona I tried to avoid him. I assumed that he didn't look forward to seeing me at all. Furthermore, I feared that the meeting might lead to some ridiculous scene, particularly if other people were present. I knew that he was fairly reclusive, that he had taken a leave from the university and spent long periods of time in his parents' hometown in Lérida. Enric remained his companion, although rumor had it that Rafel's penchant for young male prostitutes grew stronger every day.

After his death Enric and Venancio came to see me. Venancio knew the story of the translations but not that *The Mirrors* had been written entirely by me. Even so, he begged me not to tell anyone, to keep the secret in any event. Recansens—he always referred to him by his last name—had been buried with every honor due to a national poet. By then he was an unquestionable inspiration in the struggle to revive our mother tongue, and Venancio wasn't going to let my or anyone else's animosity stand in the way. If I said a word he, who knew Rafel at least as well as I did, and, furthermore, was a prestigious critic, would deny it. Besides—and he dropped this slyly—there was still the question of my possible award.

Enric nodded with a contrite expression. Despite his new glasses and slightly more defeated look, he still had the air of favorite son-in-law of a flamboyant butcher in La Boqueria—with all due respect to the profession and to the noblest of all food markets in Barcelona.

Before he left he gave me a letter that Rafel, just a few hours prior to his death, had asked him to forward to me. I debated whether to read it or not, because I feared off-handed remarks. Finally, I found the necessary courage in a bottle of bourbon. Rafel gave a painstakingly detailed account of certain circumstances of my life in South America, which no one could have possibly told him about, and resurrected forgotten experiences that, summoned by his words, gained full meaning, as if he had also taken part in them. "That's why," he said, "I have accepted the gift of your poem, of our best poem, without further ado." Rafel, in a kind of visionary delirium written down only two days before he stuffed his stomach with pills, was convinced that we were part of the same being, of the same person, and alluded to Plato's *Banquet* and to Aristophanes' theory.[14] *The Mirrors* had simply confirmed what he already knew. My poem summed up everything he wanted to contribute to literature, everything he wanted to write. And he concluded by assuring me that the most intense, fulfilling moment of his life, that splendidly drunken night in my study, he owed to me.

I even suspected that the letter might be an effective ploy on Rafel's part to stay, to perpetuate himself inside me with greater intensity, if anything, than when we lived separately. Since his death I've been feeling a terrible void that, far from diminishing with time, grows more pronounced. And I often wonder why, loving and hating each other as if we were the same person, we could not understand that the line by Baudelaire we so enjoyed to quote wasn't a simple literary pretext, but something more profound and fateful that would haunt us like the shadow does the body.

I hope that from now on no one will speculate again with possible versions of our story. On behalf of both of us, and for very good reasons, I have the last word.

Barcelona, Winter 1989

NOTES

1. Juan José Millás is a contemporary Spanish novelist who regularly contributes to *El País*, the leading Spanish newspaper that appears here under the fictitious name of *The Grand Daily Newspaper*.

2. The narrator refers to the winning side in the Spanish Civil War (1936–1939). He implies that his family is better off than Rafel's because it supports the dictatorship of Francisco Franco that followed the war and remained in power until 1975. The fraternal rivalry in the story mirrors the rivalry between the two factions that fought against each other.

3. Charles Baudelaire was one of the most influential French poets in the early twentieth century. Riera takes as the title of this story the last verse from the opening poem of Baudelaire's most famous work, *The Flowers of Evil: "Hypocrite lecteur, mon semblable, mon frère."* (Hypocritical reader, my double, my brother). These words are the key to the story.

4. Four major twentieth-century Spanish poets: Riba and Carner wrote in Catalan; Machado and Lorca, who was also a playwright, in Castilian.

5. "The delights of France."

6. Further along in the story the narrator's name appears as "José Ignacio Díaz de Benjumea," while Rafel

in his dedication calls him "my dear José Joaquín." This contradiction is part of a crucial wordplay. "José Joaquín" was the Christian name of nineteenth-century Spanish critic and newspaper editor José Joaquín de Mora. He translated Cecilia Böhl de Faber's novel *La gaviota* (The Seagull) from the original French into Spanish and subsequently published it. *La gaviota* became widely known as a Spanish novel by "Fernán Caballero," Cecilia Böhl de Faber's pen name. Böhl de Faber was a Spaniard born in France and educated in Germany, just as Rafel—an exile from the Civil War—is a Catalan raised in France who writes in French and is then translated into his own language. Böhl de Faber's linguistic dependence on José Joaquín de Mora parallels that of Rafel on his rival and friend. This also explains why in this same paragraph the narrator calls Rafel "Fernán," thus likening him to Böhl de Faber.

7. In this reference to *The Seagull* there is a pun with the Spanish word *pluma*, "quill," meaning "feather" but also "pen."

8. Ramón de Campoamor was a nineteenth-century Spanish romantic poet.

9. T.S. Eliot was a major early twentieth-century British poet born in the United States. He admired Baudelaire and in his greatest poem, *The Wasteland*, quoted the lines "mon semblable, mon frère." The "Parisian *semblable*" is, of course, Baudelaire, whose literary bond with Eliot reflects, once again, the relationship between the narrator and Rafel.

10.   Ausiàs March was the first important poet to write in Catalan. He lived in the fifteenth century. Salvador Espriu was a prominent twentieth-century Catalan poet and novelist.

11.   *Espineles* are ten-line poems.

12.   "Quinquín" is a diminutive of the character's name, Enric.

13.   Vicente Aleixandre was a twentieth-century poet who won the Nobel Prize.

14.   In the section of Plato's symposium known as "The Banquet," Aristophanes expounds his theory about the primeval man. Zeus, in order to curtail man's strength and arrogance, divided him into two. Since then each half has been desperately seeking to become reunited with the other.

Against Love in Company

SHE WAS BORN IN ARGELERS[1] on a summer afternoon. To name her Coral Flora Gaudiosa was a matter of taste, not of obligation. They didn't realize that, by doing so, they saved her from eventually having to find a pen name in order to enter her first literary contests, for everyone would assume that such a bizarre name was made up.

From her mother she inherited a sweet tooth and the body of a Rubensian goddess; from her father, a pair of fiery eyes and the gift of poetry. At age three she surprised the refugees in Argelers with patriotic couplets, which at seven she recited upon request at the reunions of exiles who arrived in Mexico. Her reputation as a poet in the Catalan colony encouraged her to aim for the Golden Rose in the newly restored poetry contest. For the occasion she wrote an ardent patriotic sonnet, highly praised by her father, and for twenty continuous nights she ruined her eyes making a black velvet dress that she planned to wear, if she won, at the celebration party. But she didn't win. A year later she tried for the Golden Violet, with identical results. Far from giving up, at the third opportunity she submitted poems for three prizes. In her most ambitious dreams she saw herself as a high priestess of the poetic art.

While waiting for the jury's decision, she started to diet. She starved herself and at the same time tried to let out the dress she hadn't yet worn. Finally she managed to get into it the day before the verdict. When she heard the news she cried: She didn't even receive a wretched honorable mention. A week later, thanks to a friend of her father who was a typist and kept in close contact with the Catalan circles in Switzerland, she found out that she had come close to winning the Golden Violet; what a shame that, at the last minute, two members of the jury deemed her poem too *risqué* and voted against it.

This tidbit, however, made her so happy that she decided to have a celebration. She took time off from the tailor's shop in exchange for working overtime another day, and threw a party. She welcomed her guests with her body literally stuffed in her dress, her teutonic rather than Catalan shape bursting out of the low neckline (perhaps this geographic and biological deviation could be explained by the Barcelonians' fondness for Wagner, since the international premiere of *Lohengrin*, previously performed only once, in Bayreuth, Germany, had taken place in the Liceu Theater in Barcelona). In a voice that, like the dress, was velvety and dark, she surprised the audience with an extremely passionate poem wrapped in blank, almost perfect decasyllabic verses. Applause, though, was not unanimous: shy and demure on the part of the ladies, much more enthusiastic on the part of their husbands, who glimpsed in those lines possibilities they had never attained.

That same afternoon she received a bouquet of roses with a request for a date, addressed to Coral Flora (nobody used her third name, Gaudiosa, imposed by her mother, either to pay tribute to her Aragonese origins or to soften a little her husband's radical secularism).

Wearing the same dress, her eyes brighter than ever, she sat down at the Cafe Colombia, not far from *La Plaza de Las Tres Culturas*. After an hour she got tired of waiting and went back home, wondering why somebody who didn't keep his word would waste money on flowers. Three days later a boy brought her a dove in a golden cage, with this brief message: "Give it your love."[2] In the Catalan colony only Albert Masdeu i Batista was known as an amateur ornithologist. This fact was a hint to Coral, who poured her energy on a batch of poems about the properties of doves. At the first opportunity, she called another meeting of exiles to check Masdeu's reactions and draw the logical conclusions. But as the intended recipient listened to the poems he showed obvious symptoms of boredom, yawning a couple of times and whispering to the person beside him, oblivious to the grand finale in which the white dove is compared to the sweet homeland, humiliated and imprisoned.

No question about it: the gift hadn't come from Masdeu. Coral Flora rejoiced: after all, the fact that Masdeu was married would have complicated things. Despite her decision to devote herself to poetry, she wanted a family, like every decent girl. In the community, however, there were only two bachelors: Baixeres, the typist, and Roger Garrolera, who was supposedly mixed up in some dishonorable business.

A week later she received a letter from Mexico City dated three days earlier. It was typed, single-spaced, free of typos or mistakes, suggesting an educated person. Someone who signed with the name *The Piper of Tapultepec* offered her eternal love, love beyond death, and likened the dove to the hand of the poetess that some day would alight upon his genitals, which were awaiting it with turgid eagerness.

Coral Flora decided not to share the content of the letter with her parents because, no doubt, they would have forced her to repudiate it. Thus, without the benefit of their possible insights, she eagerly plunged into her poetic activity. By the crack of dawn she had composed a number of lewd sonnets that she deemed acceptable, although the tercets were perhaps a trifle shrill. Before going to work, she chose the one she judged to be the most accomplished and suggestive, and addressed it to her admirer's post office box.

The anxiety of waiting was aggravated by the fact that, besides the understandable excitement of the first and—who knows—perhaps definitive love adventure, in her present state she felt a greater urge to eat. In ten days she put on almost fifty pounds, which, added to the ones she had previously accumulated, totaled two hundred and twenty-six; although she was 5'8" tall and her weight was evenly distributed, it was too much. Usually she kept a box of chocolates beside her when she wrote poetry; lately she had been spending many nights writing poems to be mailed the next day, and then waiting for them to work the desired effect and to elicit an answer. But Coral's suitor had vanished after he received the first sonnet.

At last, nearly two months later, the mail brought a letter from "The Piper" explaining the reasons for his silence: to awaken in her the need to write a poem, to spur her desire until it materialized in poetic lines. The strategy irritated Coral, so accomplished by now that writing erotic poems was child's play to her and didn't upset her at all. That's why this time she decided to send him an ultimatum: either they meet in person or she would devote herself exclusively to religious poetry.

The reply came quickly through the telegraph: "Cafe Colombia, 7:00 P.M. Dress in black." Coral tried to squeeze back into the velvet dress. It was to no avail:

as she struggled with it, she ripped the seams and burst the zipper. Sobbing, she picked up a new light pink blouse with puffy sleeves that made her look younger and more naive than black did. Just as well, she thought, now he would understand she wasn't going to cater to his every whim. Although she suspected that he would guess the truth: that she was too fat to fit into the dress. I'll lose weight, she promised herself sitting by the door of the Cafe Colombia in front of a double scoop of ice-cream spiked with liqueur, five minutes before her rendezvous. But once again he wasn't on time. Fifteen minutes later Martí Baixeres, who had been playing dominos with his friends as he did every evening, approached her.

"Allow me to invite you," he said with great formality. "If I didn't know you're waiting for someone I'd ask you if I may sit down . . ."

"Please, do," she said, pulling up a chair. "How do you know somebody stood me up?" she asked with disappointment.

"I saw you as soon as you came in. I was playing with my friends, over there. Your poems are wonderful, my child; if you just allowed me . . ."

"What?" Coral asked eagerly.

"To publish them," the typist, who had his own print shop, suggested.

"With pleasure," she said, blushing. "I'll be delighted. The problem is that I don't have any copies. I sent all the originals to a friend to see if he liked them, and he hasn't returned them yet . . ."

Martí Baixeres looked at her on the verge of ecstasy.

"You should ask for them back," he said as he got up to leave, incapable of telling her that he had already printed the proofs.

"Stay, please," she asked, suddenly understanding everything.

"You said you were waiting for somebody . . . I wouldn't want to be in the way."

"Not anymore," she reassured him, softening the astonishment reflected in her sheepish eyes. "As for the black dress you like, I'll tell you the truth: it doesn't fit. I'll lose weight, if you like."

"It's the last thing I want, my sweet. I like you just the way you are. I like you so much I could kiss you forever," Martí said with wild excitement, as if he had lost his wits. "Tomorrow and not a day later I'll talk to your father. . . You don't know how I've been longing for this moment. . . . Tell me, will you let me make you happy?"

Coral Flora smiled obligingly and gratefully. Martí Baixeres could be trusted. He admired her as a poetess, made pretty good money, and was single. It could have been a lot worse.

The entire Catalan colony gathered for the wedding. The bridegroom was pushing seventy, even if he didn't look it. The bride hadn't turned eighteen yet. The bridegroom's advanced age, however, seemed to pose no problem for Coral. She had poured her youthful, unbridled passion onto the pages of her book, which had been published by Martí and distributed among the guests as a souvenir: "When you possess me," she had written on the first page, "one hundred mares run through my veins, and the universe penetrates me like stardust."

Regardless of what these lines may suggest, Coral Flora was a virgin when she married. Martí Baixeres— a good anarchist and, therefore, a vegetarian and a strict ecologist—respected her body as he would that of a protected walrus, trying to save as much energy as possible while he prepared for a top performance on the wedding night. She, on the other hand, had plenty to burn; but, despite the uninhibited quality of her poems, she appeared shy and withdrawn, waiting for him to finally release through her veins the mares of her poem and ride beyond the limits of night.

Martí Baixeres fulfilled his duties as a husband somewhat hastily and soon fell asleep in his wife's arms, asking her to go on reciting her obscenities. Suddenly, in the wee hours of her wedding night, Coral Flora found out that she possessed the most powerful imagination in the world, but that her intuition was no bigger than that of a mosquito. Through the subsequent nights she had time to ascertain that in her realization there wasn't the slightest possibility of error. Martí Baixeres, having asked her to recite her aphrodisiac lines, usually collapsed after a single, brief tremor that always failed to stir her, even if she was at the epicenter of it.

With some trepidation she approached her mother, who comforted her with kind words: Her situation wasn't at all unusual.

Nine months into her marriage Coral Flora had a baby boy who inherited her frightened eyes and his father's Jewish nose. She wrote a string of poems for him on the subject of motherhood and made the Indian nanny memorize them, so that she could sing them to the newborn as if they were lullabies.

Disregarding her husband's insistence that she return to erotic poetry, Coral Flora protested that she had no time or desire to do so. To run the house and take care of the baby was too big a job. She lacked the peace a writer needs and so, understandably, she was in a bad mood.

Martí Baixeres felt even more restless than his wife. "Perhaps I've disappointed her in bed," he thought, torturing himself and, at the same time, refusing to admit it, "and that's why she doesn't write poems anymore. She doesn't want to lie to me."

That same afternoon he suggested that she go on vacation to the coast. "When you miss me you'll write," he said. "That's the only solution."

Coral Flora, the baby, and the Indian nanny moved to a little cabin in Cancun. The change proved to be very good for the child and also improved his mother's spirits. Early in the morning, she would wake up and stroll along the beach, although these walks stimulated in her the voracity of an unhappy fat woman.

At sundown she watched the fishermen mend nets, noticing their young muscles with delight. Sometimes she even indulged in wet dreams that, so far, had been realized only between the lines of her poems. More than once she tried to make a pass at them, but they didn't pay any attention. "I look like a frigate," she told herself, "probably they're afraid of me." But even that was no incentive to give up sweets or the little treats she was always munching. Often, however, in her dreams, she saw herself possessed by the fishermen, but she could never feel the voluptuous pleasures her poems captured so vividly. "I must be frigid," she concluded one afternoon, as she awoke up from her nap. That very evening she started a long erotic poem, which she express-mailed to her husband in installments. Written in blank verse, it was the confession of a girl separated from her lover and burning with desire. It filled Martí Baixeres with joy. As soon as he received the last fragment, he rushed to publish it. He wanted the book to be ready on the day of Coral's return.

She came back from Cancun with redder cheeks, a more frightened expression in her eyes and a new kind of restlessness. The book's success reached beyond the Catalan colony all the way into Barcelona, where it received praise from no less than *Golden Ridge*, the magazine from Montserrat, which saluted her as the new Alfonsina Storni of her country.[3] Nevertheless, her anxiety persisted, perhaps because she knew all too well that her poetry dealt in phoney and stolen merchandise.

It was nothing but a fraud, pure and simple, a fraud that she inflicted on herself every day under pressure from her husband, whom she was beginning to hate.

At that time she weighed close to three-hundred and thirty pounds and had trouble getting around. All day long she sat on a custom-made rocker, eating candy and hoping that something different and definitive would take place. Martí Baixeres had been diagnosed with a rather advanced prostate cancer. "I'm so sorry I can't make you happy, my sweet," the poor man repeated on his deathbed.

The widow dressed in strict mourning and had her son's tiny garments dyed black. Her husband had left her everything, as long as she didn't remarry. Coral Flora had no alternative but to take charge of the print shop and supervise the workers. The activity was highly beneficial to her and subdued her obsessions. She remained fat and without lovers.

One night, after an exhausting day, she locked herself in her room and studied her naked body in the mirror while she undressed. It reminded her of a Rubens Venus, and she found it attractive. "It's for no one," she thought, lying on her bed and reciting her old poems as she used to do for Martí Baixeres. Between line and line, she began to caress herself. She saw her nipples rise at the touch of her fingertips, which she ran with great deliberation along her ample thighs; her excited fingers paused to undo the curls of her mound, and exactly at the right moment, her hand slid into the crevice and she took herself unhesitatingly. Gloating on her achievement, she finally fell asleep, as she wondered at her own skill that for so many years had remained hidden.

After that night she nursed her hand with a thousand ointments and always used gloves. In love with herself, at peace with the world, she had discovered the joys of onanism, which she would practice till her death. She proudly saw her son grow up and in her mature age she wrote a book that caused a scandal. Its title was *Against Love in Company* and it opened with the following verses:

All the mares that run through my poems
come out of my fingers. My fingers alone
are the tigers that take me to
infinity.

Deià, Majorca, Summer 1990

NOTES

1. Argelers is the Catalan name of Argelès-sur-Mer, a small town on the Mediterranean in Southern France. During the Spanish Civil War, many people from the region of Catalonia fled to France and to Mexico, as this story reflects.

2. Lyrics of a popular Latin American song: "*Si a tu ventana llega una paloma/trátala con cariño que es mi persona.*" (If a dove comes to your window/give it your love, for it will be me.)

3. Alfonsina Storni was one of Argentina's best known twentieth-century poets.

The Seduction of Genius

São Paulo, September 1, 1990
Ms. Carmen Balcells
Literary Agency
Barcelona

*M*Y DEAR AND DISTINGUISHED FRIEND: My name used to be Juan Chamorro, but that may not ring a bell at all. In any case, I'd better start by asking you to search in your memory, for my justification for writing is that two years ago I had the pleasure of meeting you in São Paulo at a reception in the home of the mother of Nélida Piñón, a writer I greatly admire.[1]

Around that time (May, 1987) I had finished two novels that Nélida kindly read and that, given her intelligence and good judgment, she thoroughly condemned. I know she was right, because other people I consulted concurred with her and persuaded me to give up writing. Convinced that they were correct but also feeling terribly hurt, because if there is something I have always wanted, it's precisely to make a mark in the history of literature, I followed their advice. I know that the wings of genius have never even brushed my forehead; still, I lack neither imagination nor sensibility to appreciate those genuine merits that validate a work of art beyond dispute.

You probably think, Ms. Balcells, my dear Carme— I hope you won't mind if I call you Carme, as you asked me to do at that unforgettable gathering—that I, having reached this conclusion, decided to take up literary criticism. I didn't. Criticism strikes me as a futile exercise that leads nowhere. Besides, it doesn't interest me. I want more, let's say that I aim higher. If I can't create, at least I'd like to follow closely the workings of creativity, to witness the creative process from the beginning to the end, to share every minute of the life of somebody who has received from the gods the gift to fashion a world out of nothing, populate it with creatures meant to survive her and, thanks to them, gain her immortality. In exchange for being present at the performance, I offer my cooperation as secretary, corrector, clerk, typist, and even slave—to fill excess pages, of course—in addition to husband.

This way I could secure myself a place in posterity as the writer's companion, mentioned very briefly in encyclopedia articles but fully honored, no doubt, with several pages in well-documented biographies. Besides, I could play a part, no matter how modest, in a formidable task.

My mother was Catalan, my father from Valladolid, and I was born in Brazil; therefore, I have a good command of Portuguese besides Catalan and Castilian and I know the literatures in these languages very well, which encouraged me to try my luck first with my dear and admired Nélida Piñón. But she flatly turned me down. Having never considered marriage in the first place, how could she accept somebody she didn't care for at all? Nélida's refusal disappointed me, but it was no reason to give up my project.

I took advantage of a trip my parents had to make to Madrid and Barcelona and went along. In Madrid I interviewed Rosa Chacel first. I discovered her books in my adolescence and they fascinated me. Everything went smoothly till I told her about my plan. She laughed so hard she nearly choked to death. Then one Thursday I went to the Royal Academy of the Spanish Language to meet Carmen Conde, but she had flu and, at her age, her recovery was expected to be fairly slow. With Carmen Martín Gaite I was much luckier in the beginning, for in her letter she even seemed to give me some hope; but later she stopped writing and didn't show up at our rendezvous at Cafe Gijón.

From Madrid I went to Barcelona, thinking my chances would be better there. My intuition told me everything would work out in Barcelona. Esther Tusquets was delightful. We played poker for three weeks before I proposed. I had a hunch that I must proceed with extreme caution. I wasn't mistaken. As soon as I revealed my intentions she sent me away unceremoniously, after having cleaned my pockets. Anna Maria Moix, who is charming and would be even more so if she weren't in a stable relationship, introduced me to Ana María Matute. She asked me to tea and, in passing, dropped a remark that she found young boys boring and cared only about mature me . . . People told me wonderful things about Montserrat Roig, but at the time she was taking a course in the United States. You have no idea how I mourned Mercè Rodoreda once again, and how much I would have liked, at least, to try with her.[2] I assure you I never envied so much the luck of Carmen Llera, Marina Castaño, and Asunción Mateo, not to speak of María Kodama . . . To me, Borges will always be the greatest.[3]

One evening, shortly before returning to Brazil, I was walking along Moll de la Fusta in Barcelona with Anna Maria Moix. As we talked about María Kodama —a real obsession of mine—I realized that, if I really wanted to fulfill my wish above anything else, I had only one option. I revealed it to my friend and we hugged each other, crying, in the middle of the boardwalk.

The surgery, my dear Carme, has been a success. I feel completely happy, like a new person. Actually, I am a new person. A person capable of setting in motion all the trappings of feminine seduction without embarrassment. That's why I'm positive that in the end I will achieve my purpose. How wonderful, to be sweet, flirtatious, and spoiled all at once! Perhaps I always wanted to be a woman and just didn't know.

The doctors who dealt with me are all sweethearts. They say that in a week I'll be able to leave the hospital and that the results of the operation have been spectacularly positive. Not only have I become a woman on the outside and in the inside, but my degree of femininity grows by the minute. I can feel it. From one woman to another I confess, my dear, that before the operation I groaned at the thought of having to wear chest suspenders, whereas now I find a bra an extremely sexy accessory. I don't look bad in front of the mirror, and I believe that with my make-up on I can almost compete with the admired wives of my admired geniuses.

In sum, dear Carme, Anna Maria Moix assured me you wouldn't mind if I wrote to you; she also suggested that, before I make a decision, I talk to you because, no doubt, you can give me very good advice. I'm just a happy woman following instructions; do you realize how quickly I've adjusted?

On the 25th, if everything goes as planned, I'll leave for Barcelona. To even the score with Nélida I won't say goodbye to her, so that she can't see how gorgeous the doctors made me. I hope you can give me an appointment as soon as I arrive. Let me forward you a list of my preferences: José Luis Sampedro, Juan García Hortelano, Juan Benet. Juan Marsé, Manolo Vázquez Montalbán, and Eduardo Mendoza may be too young. Do you know Pere Calders? And his broth-

er-in-law, Tísner? With his pirate look I find him fasci-
nating. What about Perucho? What a hunk! I'm ruling
out Gabriel García Márquez on account of Mercedes
(I know her well, she would scratch my eyes out),
Sábato (my charms would be wasted on him) and, alas!
Mario Vargas Llosa.[4]

 With complete confidence in your willingness
to help, I send you all my sisterly affection.

      JUANITA CHAMORRO
      Barcelona, September 1990

NOTES

1. Nélida Piñón is a contemporary Brazilian writer.

2. These are the names of prominent contemporary women novelists in Spain, except Nélida Piñón, mentioned earlier, who is from Brazil.

3. Names of famous writers' wives. María Kodama is Borges' widow.

4. Names of major contemporary writers from Spain and Latin America. Mercedes is García Márquez's wife; as for the remark that the narrator's charms would be wasted on Ernesto Sábato, it alludes to the blindness of the well-known Argentinean novelist.

Report

$\mathcal{D}$ELMIRA ALONSO SAMBLANCAT (Santa Perpétua de Moguda, Barcelona 1951–Gerona 2010) began her literary career in 1972 with the short novel *He Comes to See Me Some Afternoons* that soon made her famous. This work was followed by *He Came to See Me Monday* (1973), which, in the view of experts [sic] confirmed her narrative talent, *Why Don't You Come to See Me?* (1975), *Let Me Know if You Can't Come* (1979), and *I No Longer Want You to Come* (1983). The latter closes her quintet, which evolves around the strange relationship between a businessman and his old, experienced wet nurse at the time of the so-called *transition* (1975–1995).

In addition to these novels, she published a book of poems, *Windstorm* (1987), and in her mature years wrote what everyone considers to be her masterpiece, *Don't Be Late, or I'll Die* (1995); in my opinion, it is but a rehash of her former texts, riddled with mistakes, inside jokes, and tributes to other authors, the kind of thing turn-of-the-century critics used to call intertextuality and we call plagiarism.

My exhaustive research into her life has yielded an abundance of data (see appendix 1, microfiches 1.1, 1.2), as well as a fair amount of graphic materials. Throughout her almost thirty-year-long literary career she was photographed approximately five hundred and twenty-five times at conferences, literary parties, panels of judges, award-giving ceremonies, and book signings. We have, therefore, a splendid and detailed record of her aging process.

Similarly, we know that she was interviewed forty-five times by the national TV station (fifteen in cultural programs and the rest in recreational and variety shows, cuisine lessons, and trivia contests) and twenty-five times by private stations, among which she didn't have as many fans or friends. She took part in two hundred and twenty-one round tables, attended one hundred and five writers' gatherings, presented fifteen original papers and read the same paper on her life and work, with minor variations, one hundred and eight times. Together with other colleagues, she signed twenty-five pamphlets (the media featured nineteen of them). Since the coming of democracy she always supported the party in power, although she refrained from joining it. In the early days she was a feminist.

She traveled around Europe and America at least on twenty occasions and received three literary prizes: the Josep Pla Award for *He Comes to See Me Some Afternoons*

(1972), the Prudenci Bertrana Award for *Let Me Know if You Can't Come* (1979), and the Golden Ridge Criticism Award for *I No Longer Want You to Come* (1983).

As for her private life, I have been able to prove that she married twice (1971 and 1987), had three lovers (1972–1975),(1989–2000), and (2000–2010) and seventy-six *flings*, which is the word used at the time for casual copulation (see appendix 3, microfiches 3.1, 3.2, 3.3, 3.4).

Her first marriage produced two children, Delmir (1972–2030) and Agustina (1973–2040), who showed no literary inclinations at all. Her first husband's name was Carles Borromeu Pascual (Sóller, Majorca 1947–Barcelona 2020). He worked at a branch of March Bank and shared with his wife's first lover, Antoni Massutí i Passareu (San Pol de Mar, Barcelona 1951–Palafrugell, Gerona 2000) the dedications of her first three books.

After divorcing Borromeu she married Pere Antoni Pessarrodona i Vilaquadrada (Barcelona 1942–Santa Coloma de Farners, Gerona 2000) in a civil court. He was an entomologist and a socialist who had been engaged in a tempestuous relationship with the wife of the nation's president (see appendix 4, microfiche 1.2). As for Angel León Pérez (Salamanca 1945–Madrid 2000), we may consider him a beneficiary of her second marriage, since he appears to have been not only the writer's lover but also her husband's, whose homosexual leanings were known to everyone. The Acquired

Immuno-Deficiency Syndrome—very much like tuberculosis in the romantic period—ended the lives of both
Pessarrodona and Léon within three hours of each
other. It was a devastating blow for Delmira. Three
years later she started to live with Antón Carrión Béjar
(Murcia 1952–Madrid 2020), who survived her by ten
years and, after Delmira's death, took it upon himself
to sort out her correspondence and files. His scrupu-
lous work has made my work considerably easier.

Although after ten months of research I have grown
rather fond of Delmira Alonso Samblancat, I believe
that her life was hopelessly uninteresting and not in the
least exceptional. It seems cut after the same pattern as
those of her more or less prestigious colleagues at the
close of the twentieth century. Therefore, I don't think
that, given its doubtful relevance, the company should
embark on the costly enterprise of publicizing her biog-
raphy in the form of animated cartoons; neither do I
advise wasting money on an adaptation to comic strips.

I request permission to resume from now on my
research on Maria Duran Pocovi (Barcelona 1954–
Barcelona 2010), whose life, I suspect, might offer us
some interesting surprises, perhaps even the revelation
of a morbid secret, for she never appeared on public
occasions, was rarely photographed and, as far as I
know, always lived with the same person, all of which
renders her behavior truly odd. Maybe she had some
physical handicap. It seems, moreover, that she didn't
live the life of a writer: She simply wrote.

Surprise at Sri Lanka

*O*N HER BIRTHDAY, August 29, she gave herself a trip to Sri Lanka. She deserved it. All through the year she had worked very hard: three journalistic books, over fifty articles, and thirteen scripts for a television series, two of which she hadn't finished yet. Besides, she had a hunch that the trip would not only be relaxing but, as her horoscope predicted, would bring a pleasant surprise, something more serious and permanent—her intuition told her—than a casual one night stand with any tourist in a hotel.

The golden age of her second, sizzling youth that had followed her divorce was now far behind. She had almost forgotten the faces and names of her provisional partners in her frantic nights as a liberated girl, who in the seventies had worn hippie clothes and gone through her rite of passage in a sweet, communal initiation on a beach in Formentera. Often, however, she still felt a sharp longing for youthful caresses on the skin that time had mistreated.

Lately she spent long hours reminiscing about how she had put an end to that erotic frenzy and decided she could no longer afford the supply of whisky required for the proverbial "nightcap"; more and more her apartment resembled the Marx Brothers' stateroom scene in *A Night at the Opera* and among her regular visitors there were, sometimes, even policemen. Filled with nostalgia, she browsed all too often through albums of newspaper clippings with interviews and news about herself. Most of them belonged to the period when she published her thoroughly documented historical essay on men's underwear, *Apollo in Briefs*, that remained the top best seller for twelve continuous months.

To be the official expert in a subject of such socio-economic and—why not?—political significance made her a necessary presence at every cultural event in the country. She felt obligated to teach seminars in international summer courses at various universities and to socialize with sectors of the old intelligentsia, the jet set, and other beautiful people. In four different seasons she served as a member of the jury in the Mister Tong and Mister Costa Brava contests, and attended every event, soiree, and wild party that came her way. She even designed a very successful unisex undergarment, christened with the name *pantyslip*, that a large company in Sabadell decided to market.

In the early days of the transition to democracy she reached the peak of her good fortune. Every women's magazine in the country, with the exception of *Dove* (the editor rightly considered her articles out of keeping with the pious nature of the publication, although in truth she couldn't wait for a piece on the underpants supposedly worn by Saint Peter) wanted to hire her as a reporter. Two weekly journals of political news offered her permanent engagements; she wasn't definitively anointed, however, until she signed an exclusive contract with the *Grand Daily Newspaper* as director of the Sunday supplement on trivia, gossip, chit-chat, and miscellaneous topics.

But all that came to an end fifteen years ago. At this point, even though she kept very busy, her market value had decreased considerably. She made plenty of money but had to accept far too many jobs. In the old days, one was enough to make a fancy living and to give her a stimulating taste of power.

Traffic between her sheets had also slowed down considerably, but this didn't bother her too much. After all, she had always boasted that it was she who picked her casual lovers, and the literati, journalists, and celebrities that she bedded all came out of the same cookie cutter; she knew all too well the rules of their boring games.

Every other day she had to fight a guilty conscience for having been a liberated woman of the extinct variety. Deep inside and despite herself, rooted in her petit bourgeois morality, which she hadn't been able to stifle completely, lay the anxiety that perhaps she wasn't exactly a liberated woman, but a *demi-mondaine* free of charge. She would have gladly given up both labels in exchange for a stable partner and, most of all, a sensible marriage. A hunch told her it was still possible. All she had to do was concentrate on this goal and use every means available. Besides, the horoscope also seemed to be on her side.

She picked some flattering clothes, bought a truckload of creams and moisturizers and climbed on a plane, hoping that fate would do its work. Immediately she realized that among her traveling companions not one fulfilled the necessary requirements to be a candidate. All of them were couples, except for a guy who looked like he had just gotten a divorce and would hit on the first native teenage girl to come around. "Better this way," she thought; "if this is going to be a clean break and a new beginning, I'd rather have a native. At least he'll be more exotic."

In the first week nothing interesting happened. The hotel was tolerably posh and she spent long hours relaxing by the pool. She still had five days left and everything was possible, although she was psyching herself up to accept that in all likelihood nothing would develop. Life had been quite generous to her, and she'd better face once and for all her image in the mirror and the loneliness of her mature age, giving up forever her dark, secret longings for the corny happiness of marriage.

It happened one afternoon in the hotel's boutique two days before she left. She was buying presents and felt two eyes staring at the back of her head. As she turned around she thought that they glared like burning embers, and drew a smile of complicity. Later, when he walked up to her and stood in her way, she knew that it was the unique opportunity she had been waiting for, despite the fact that he seemed no older than twenty and could have been her son.

"I'd like to buy you a drink," he said in fairly fluent English. "I'm sorry to jump on you like this, but I know you're going back to your country soon and I won't have a chance to spend time with you unless I take the initiative. I've seen you often these days because I'm a guide and I pick up tourists at the hotel . . . I know you're a journalist."

"Happy to meet you," she said, and she really was happy to be picked up in such a candid, old-fashioned way . . . "Maybe he'll ask me for money," she thought. "He's too good-looking . . ."

But none of that happened. On the contrary. He didn't allow her to pay for a single drink and took her to the best restaurants in town, besides showing her everything, from the funkiest districts to the most refined private clubs reserved for millionaires. He was more than delightful. He exuded delicacy and charm and insisted that he preferred mature women with class to American teenagers who instantly tried to seduce him. Most of all, he enjoyed the company of intelligent people, and she was unquestionably an intelligent woman. That job as a guide brought in some extra money, but his real goal was to be a journalist, like her; that's why in the winter he attended the university. Those few hours with her, he insisted, weren't enough for him either, and he promised to maintain a stable relationship in the future:

"I have chosen you, you're my candidate," he told her, trying to sound tough, but kissing her right away with a tenderness she had forgotten. Nonetheless, she replied that in her view it was fate that had led her to him and explained that his name was written in her horoscope. He smiled cryptically and drank to her good fortune.

The last night the guide patiently honed his skills and took her over and over to the point of exhaustion. She repeated in a trance her favorite lines by Cernuda,[1] which she had never shared with anyone: "I don't want freedom/but the freedom of being imprisoned in someone/whose name I cannot utter without shivering," even though in English they sounded terrible. At the crack of dawn, a few hours before her plane flight, he left the bedroom, after promising that he would pay her a visit as soon as he could. Incapable of going back to sleep, she got up and finished packing. She felt so happy, so reconciled with life, that she even took the time to answer the hotel survey designed to improve as much as possible the quality of service. She gave the top ratings to almost every question. Then glanced at a leaflet that was inside an envelop with her name written on it and that she hadn't noticed at first. It explained that she had been randomly chosen to participate in a raffle among the most distinguished customers of the five star hotel. The prize was to have a private guide at her disposal for two days and two nights, in order to make her visit to Sri Lanka even more pleasurable.

Barcelona, September 1990

NOTE

1. Luis Cernuda was a member of the group of Spanish poets known as the Generation of 1927.

Recipe Book

$\mathcal{I}$ TELL IT LIKE IT IS, Antonieta, just like it is. . . .
Really disgusting. . . . Believe me, I still don't get it. I
wish I hadn't listened to this editor, or whatever they
call him, but, tell me, how could I imagine a sweet deal
like this one could leave such a bitter taste? I was a real
sucker. I didn't ask no questions, just said yes right
away, I'd look for the notebook and the rest of them
notes scattered in my drawers, and I signed up a
receipt for an advance, never suspectin' nothing. . . .
Like I say, a real sucker, but then, what else was there
to do? Would you have smelled the rat? Besides,
money is always a come-on. Even though my hubby,
thank the Lord, left me enough to live comfortably,
a little help with the funeral is always appreciated; but
more than the dough, Antonieta, what meant a lot to
me was the thought that on account of this he'd be
better remembered. . . . If the book gets published he'll
be remembered alright, but not for the right reasons!

And there ain't no stoppin' it, for, I ask you: What do I say to this guy when he shows up in the afternoon to pick up the stuff? That the crew that whitewashed my walls stole the notebook? That they dumped all them papers? I, stupid me, told him myself I'd look after it like my life depended on it! Oh, no, not a chance! He wouldn't fall for it for a minute! Even if I had somebody rewrite the whole thing in a new notebook, changin' whatever I saw fit, he'd see the monkey business on the very first page. . . . My hubby had already showed him these notes and, with the intention of publishin' them before his last setback, he started writin' them all over again. . . . This character knows very well what he's up to and where he puts his money. It won't be easy to pull the wool over his eyes, no sir . . . He won't come alone neither, he'll bring his lawyer or God knows who, with them papers ready for me to sign . . . I've gone too far to pull out of it now and these people who handle law suits, Antonieta, scare the livin' daylights out of me and make me all tongue-tied.

Who could have thought just a few hours ago, when I proudly imagined my husband's name in print and his picture, like Senyora Coloma's, on the front page, that now I'd give my right arm to take it all back? Come to think of it, if I hadn't been so taken in with the idea, I should've known there was somethin' fishy when the editor, while he wrote the receipt, asked me, as cool as a cucumber, to find a picture of a girl in skimpy clothes to put next to the one of Bernat in his uniform and chef's hat . . . I didn't think nothing of it . . . I innocently told him it seemed more natural to show him with a fruit basket or some fowl hangin' from a hook . . . It'll be the talk of the town, Antonieta. . . . Everybody and his mother will buy the book when they see it on display in the stores. Of course, I was the first to break the news to every Tom, Dick, and Harry that there's a book comin' out with them recipes left by my husband, rest in peace. To tell you the truth, no one was surprised, 'cause you know very well, Antonieta, that the hotels in Palma have seen few master chefs who spent so many years as he did cookin' in Marseilles and gettin' his whiskers scorched in Paris restaurants . . . French cookin' had no secrets for him.

But, what do you know. . . .This man who fixed the fanciest soufflés and marinated red meat so it hardly took no cookin' time at all, and then dressed it with butter sauce and those mushrooms pigs dig out of the ground with their snouts and folks rave about, he was crazy for my concoctions. "You have a knack for it like nobody else," the rascal used to say till his dyin' moments. Now me, to be perfectly honest, I never tried more than a couple of his dishes, for I didn't go near the hotels, and at home—you know how men are—he didn't stick his nose in the kitchen even to boil vegetables . . . Don't you think it didn't make me happy to be his favorite. . . . I was even grateful, really, 'cause after all it was a good thing his stews didn't touch our kitchenware . . . Nothing but my cookin' 'til the very end.

Yes, Antonieta, 'til the very end . . . I want to tell you about this too, even if you say I'm nuts to make a big deal of it . . . the thing is, it's been eatin' me since my husband kicked the bucket; at least, if I tell you about it, I'll feel better, otherwise this whole business will drive me crazy . . . I feel guilty, honey; I fear I tried so hard to satisfy his whims that perhaps I sent him to heaven a little quicker than the Lord intended . . . No kiddin', don't tell me it don't make sense . . . His passion for my stews may've given him the last push. Not that I didn't warn him: "Bernat, it's gonna make you sick, there'll be plenty of rabbit with onions when you're better," but he, stubborn as a mule, "Come on, now, I'm not gonna recover from this one. Don't you see my days are over?" And me, fool that I was, I was almost flattered. "But, Bernat, what will the doctor say if he finds out?" and he, poor soul, "Let him say whatever he pleases, he ain't on his last legs yet. Are you gonna take this away from me, just when I'm about to leave this world?" And I ask you, Antonieta, what would you have done in my place, seein' him in pain and with a foot in the next world? I skipped the cherry pepper and the pinch of spices, and I made sure there weren't no bones left and everything was real smooth and easy to swallow . . . And, wouldn't you know it? He coughed and turned his head . . . You can imagine how frightened I was . . . Yes, I know, it had to end one way or another . . . and maybe you're right, maybe he was better off leavin' this world with the taste of his favorite dish in his mouth . . . You won't believe me, but it's a comfort to me to hear you say it . . . The thought that maybe it was my fault has been keepin' me awake nights . . . I tell you, you have to pull a bad thought out of your head like you pull a thorn out of your finger . . .

What time is the clock ringin'? Five? My, oh my! They'll be here any time now. You've got to help me, Antonieta . . . How? What am I thinkin' of, I haven't told you yet, have I? You've got to sell to me one of them little bottles with the white stuff and the little brush, like you were usin' the other day to erase letters . . . that's right. I'll go over the notebook with a fine-tooth comb, no one can stop me from takin' out my name from all that filth. Listen to the name of this sauce: "to beautiful Maria." How do you like it? Or his last dressing: "the way Marieta likes it." You don't want to know what's in it. In this filth there's no room for my name. Nobody can hold up a candle to me when it comes to morals; the last thing I want now is for folks to think dirty just sayin' my name. At least, if there's nothing else I can do, I'll erase any trace of myself in his recipes . . . No, honey, I never dreamt what this cookin' was about, for he who does no evil thinks no evil . . . And yet, there were some signs . . . Since he retired, we hadn't spent a single Saturday watchin' TV together, and now and then he'd go out even another night in the week. "It's a gang, Maria," he said, "I cook for a few friends. Wives don't come to gang parties."

And I was happy to stay, not once suspectin' one could do something improper on a stove . . . A retired man at home dies of boredom, you know; what's wrong with goin' out for a bite with a few pals? And, believe me, friends he had plenty of . . . Why, they followed him everywhere! You saw it for yourself at the funeral: for every woman there were five men prayin' the Lord have mercy on his soul. Grateful, that's what they were . . . That's why it was no surprise when the editor, after givin' his sympathies, said to me: "The world has lost an artist, madam . . . You and I have to talk, one of these days . . . Above all, don't lose those recipes. The happiness of many men is at stake." I had tears in my eyes . . . How could I think that. . . ! When he came by last Friday with that notion of publishin' the stuff, I was hopin' I'd see Bernat's name on a street sign before my death and, thinkin' I was honorin' his memory, Antonieta, I signed my own sentence . . .

To think up to this moment I was a contented woman! I got up today with a clear head and this incredible energy to turn the house upside down . . . In the twinklin' of an eye I finished the house chores and then the thought struck me: "It's a real shame, Maria, that everybody talks about your husband's talents and you haven't got a chance to savor his sauces . . . Come on, there's still time. Do it in his memory." That's when I started browsin' through his notebook. But, I don't know, I couldn't get excited about nothing. Half of the time I couldn't figure out what he was talkin' 'bout, and when I did it didn't do no good, 'cause it either turned my stomach or called for all them exotic herbs . . . Anyway, you know me, Antonieta: when I get an idea into my head I don't let go of it easy. . . "Senyor Biel will tell me the name in Majorcan,"[1] says I to myself, "he's an expert in the matter of herbs." I curse that moment, honey! I would have lived so happy in my ignorance, with a few pennies in my pocket, even if folks laughed behind my back! Nothing worse than suddenly findin' there's egg on your face and you can't wash it off! So, "these herbs," says the rascal, "aren't my specialty. What do you want them for? Wouldn't you rather make yourself some nice soup?" The more I tried to get him to talk plain the more he hemmed and hawed, 'til in the end he gave in: "I told you, you'll only find this in specialty stores." "How come?" says I. "D'you really wanna know?" says he. "Alright. The stores that sell stuff to make men's dicks happy and strong." I thought, Antonieta, that nothing in this world could shock me. Was I wrong! I stood there frozen and dumbfounded. No smellin' salts, no rubbin' alcohol on my temples could revive me . . . For I ask you, could you ever have guessed that Bernat, at his age, thought of such things? Whoever heard of cookin' to get your buddies all worked up? An artist! . . . The rotten, filthy perverts! Take my word for it, if any of them came up here he'd go down hangin' from a rope . . . Just imagine, Antonieta, if the book is published. This husband of mine will have more fans than the Holy Christ in the cathedral . . .

I tell it like it is, Antonieta, just like it is . . .
Disgusting. I'll say one thing, though: the business of
becomin' a master at fixin' concoctions to make folks
hot I can understand, for men lose their wits when
they get to be a certain age and can't get it up no more;
what I won't forgive is misusin' my name . . . Everybody
and his brother is gonna think we were always at it in
this house and didn't make enough to keep fixin' bro-
ken bed frames . . . That, I can't have, Antonieta; me,
who always held up my chin, 'cause believe me,
Antonieta, I tell you from the bottom of my heart: If
my husband fixed these hot stews it was for other people, 'cause he, poor dear, never touched them, he only
ate my dishes, cross my heart. For the last twenty years
no cock crowed in this bed . . .

Barcelona, Winter 1985

NOTE

1. Majorcan is the variety of Catalan spoken in the Balearic Islands in the Mediterranean, where Carme Riera was born and grew up.

SELECTED BIBLIOGRAPHY

Works by Carme Riera in English Translation:

Torre, Cristina de la, trans., *Mirror Images*. New York: Peter Lang, 1993.

SECONDARY SOURCES

Bergmann, Emilie. "Letters and Diaries as Narrative Strategies in Contemporary Catalan Women's Writing." In *Critical Essays on the Literatures of Spain and Spanish America*, edited by Luis González del Valle and Julio Baena, 19–38. Boulder, Colorado: Society of Spanish and Spanish American Studies, 1991.

Johnson, Roberta. "Voice and Intersubjectivity in Carme Riera's Narratives." Ibid., 153–59.

McNerney, Kathleen, ed. *On Our Own Behalf: Women's Tales from Catalonia*. Lincoln: University of Nebraska Press, 1988. (Includes the following stories by Riera in translation: "I Leave You, My Love, the Sea as a Token," "Some Flowers," "The Knot, the Void,"

"A Cool Breeze for Wanda," and "Miss Angels Ruscadell Investigates the Horrible Death of Marianna Servera").

McNerney, Kathleen, and Enríquez de Salmanca, Cristina, eds. *Double Minorities of Spain: A Bibliographic Guide to Women Writers of the Catalan, Galician, and Basque Countries.* New York: Modern Language Association of America, 1994.

Porqueras-Mayo, Albert, et al. *The New Catalan Short Story: An Anthology.* Washington, D.C.: University Press of America, 1983.

Schumm, Sandra J. "Borrowed Language in Carme Riera's *Cuestión de amor propio.*" *Anales de la literatura española contemporánea* 20, no. 1, 2 (1995): 199–214.

Tsuchiya, Akiko. "The Paradox of Narrative Seduction in Carme Riera's *Cuestión de amor propio.*" *Hispania* 75, no. 2 (1992): 281–86.

Carme Riera is professor of Spanish literature at Autonomous University of Barcelona. She has authored several award-winning novels and short story collections in both her native language, Catalan, and in Castilian. Riera is undoubtedly one of the most prominent writers in Spain, and her works have been translated into French, German, Portuguese, Dutch, and Greek. She recently has been awarded the *Creu de Sant Jordi* (St. George's Cross), the Catalan equivalent to being knighted.

Roser Caminals-Heath is professor of Spanish literature at Hood College in Maryland. A translator and a prize-winning novelist, she is the author of *Les herbes secretes* (The Secret Herbs) and *Once Remembered, Twice Lived* (also published in Catalan as *Un segle de prodigis*).

Holly Cashman is a Ph.D. candidate in Romance Linguistics at the University of Michigan (Ann Arbor).